ANTONIA POZZI

Breath

Antonia Pozzi, 1937

A N T O N I A   P O Z Z I

Breath
Poems and Letters

Edited and Translated by
Lawrence Venuti

Wesleyan University Press
Middletown, Connecticut

WESLEYAN POETRY

Published by Wesleyan University Press,
Middletown, CT 06549

Translation, notes, and introduction © 2002 by
Lawrence Venuti. The Italian poems of Antonia
Pozzi appear courtesy of Garzanti Libri, from their
book *Parole,* ed. Alessandra Cenni and Onorina Dino,
© Garzanti Libri s.p.a. 1998, © Garzanti Editore s.p.a
1989. The Italian letters of Antonia Pozzi in this col-
lection appear courtesy of Rosellina Archinto, from
their book *L'età delle parole è finita: Lettere 1927–1938,*
© 1989 Congregazione delle Suore del Preziosissimo
Sangue di Monza, © 1989 Rosellina Archinto s.p.a.
Photographs are used by permission of Suor
Onorina Dino.

ISBN 0-8195-6543-1 cloth
ISBN 0-8195-6544-x paper

Printed in the United States of America
Designed and typeset by Julie Allred and Barbara Williams
Set in Bembo type by B. Williams and Associates

5 4 3 2 1

CiP data appear at the back of the book

FOR MARTHA TENNENT HAMILTON

L'amor que no esperaves sempre és més pur.

És un regal de compassió on el temps
Més esquerp i incert, més absolut,
Sembla aturar-se arran del teu silenci.

Saber que hi ets em fa ser
i créixer indiferent al seu poder,
obstinat davant la dalla que trenca els fils
tan prims de les nostres veles negres.

Contents

LETTERS

The Dolomites. Undated. Photograph by Antonia Pozzi.

Versions of Antonia Pozzi

She was born on 13 February 1912 into an affluent Milanese family. Her father, Roberto Pozzi, was a lawyer who in 1936 was appointed by the Fascist Party to serve as *podestà* or mayor of a Lombard village; her mother, Lina Cavagna Sangiuliani, was related to the Romantic poet Tommaso Grossi, an associate of the great nineteenth-century novelist Alessandro Manzoni.

Antonia Pozzi received the fine education that befitted her class. She attended the best schools, learned languages, studied music and art, practiced such sports as tennis, horseback riding, skiing, and mountain climbing. She visited various towns throughout Italy, especially winter and summer resorts, and traveled to England, France, Germany, Austria, Greece, and North Africa.

During the 1930s she was a member of an elite cultural circle, the friend of leading Italian writers and thinkers. At the University of Milan, she studied with the influential philosopher Antonio Banfi. Her classmates, all students of Banfi, included figures who later distinguished themselves in literary criticism (Luciano Anceschi), poetry (Vittorio Sereni), and philosophy (Enzo Paci). The thinking was modernist, in touch with recent German trends such as phenomenology and existentialism, socially engaged, and inevitably responding, in part, to the repressive, imperialistic agendas of Italian Fascism.

Under Banfi's tutelage, Pozzi wrote a thesis on Flaubert's literary development. She planned to write an ambitious historical novel about northern Lombardy, about the land and its people, starting in the 1870s and spanning three generations. She took artfully composed photographs of the Lombard countryside, the mountains and lakes, churches and fairs, the workers and the children in the villages.

In 1937 she began teaching at a Milanese technical institute and performed volunteer social work, visiting the poor and assisting in juvenile courts. A year later she underwent an appendectomy, and although she recovered, her fragile health was weakened. On 2 December 1938 her body was found on the outskirts of the city, near the abbey of Chiaravalle, in the snow. She had drugged herself and contracted pneumonia. She died the next day. The note she left behind refers to "something hidden in my nature, an illness of the nerves that deprives me of every resistance and prevents me from seeing things in a balanced way." The official report, following the family's instructions but also reflecting a request in her note, describes the cause of death as a "sudden attack." Among Pozzi's papers was found a set of notebooks that contained over three hundred poems. Her parents called this body of work "an intimate diary" that she kept "modestly hidden." Written between 1929 and 1938, the poems were known only to Pozzi's closest friends, particularly two women (Lucia Bozzi and Elvira Gandini) whom she had met in secondary school.

Pozzi's suicide at twenty-six, as well as her gender, made early critics uncomfortable, reluctant to pronounce her an important contemporary poet. So they decided that the case was moot, her talents unfulfilled. They searched for signs of "femininity" in her poems. Eugenio Montale, in a 1945 essay that became the preface to the early editions, preferred to read them as *poems* that everywhere evinced a "desire to reduce the weight of words to the minimum." And he shrewdly observed that "this desire already constitutes Pozzi's departure from the generic feminine gratuity that is the dream of so many male critics."

In 1939, within a year of Pozzi's death, her father arranged to have a substantial selection of her poetry (ninety-one texts) published privately in an edition of three hundred copies. Then in 1943, 1948, and 1964, expanded selections were issued in the prestigious series of contemporary poets created by the commercial publisher Mondadori (the series was called "Lo specchio: I poeti del nostro tempo"—the mirror, poetry seen as a reflection of its historical period). Until 1989, however, selections of Pozzi's poems were based on texts edited by her father, who was proud of his daughter's literary achievement but undoubtedly wanted to craft a respectable image of her.

From the 1939 selection, for instance, he excluded poems that are explicitly sexual, such as "Innocenza" and "Pan." In "Odore di fieno" ("Scent of hay") he revised the line "[le lacrime] tremolano nella mia anima impura" ("[tears] tremble in my impure soul") by deleting the word "impura." He deleted the phrase "Dopo il bacio" ("After the kiss") at the beginning of "L'allodola" ("The skylark"), a poem about a lovers' rendezvous. He retitled a poem to prevent any suggestion of suicide: "Fine" ("End") became first "Mare" ("Sea"), then "Imbarco" ("Embarkation"). And he removed dedications from poems addressed to her first lover, Antonio Maria Cervi, whom he opposed.

The father's control of his daughter's writing began immediately after her death. He requested her letters from correspondents and then revised and recopied them. He even edited her suicide note, striking out phrases and writing at the top of the page: "Original burned. Reconstruction from Papà's memory."

Stylistically, Pozzi's poems are representative of hermeticism (*ermetismo*), the powerful combination of precise language, dense imagery, and free verse that dominated Italian poetry from the 1920s to the 1950s. She admired the first books of the major hermetic poets: Giuseppe Ungaretti, Montale, Salvatore Quasimodo. She underlined titles and phrases in their work. She understood it in the context of international modernist trends. She read T. S. Eliot, Paul Valéry, and Rainer Maria Rilke in the original languages as well as in Italian translations.

Ermetismo was initially a pejorative label affixed by critics, a swipe at the obscurity created by the modernist form of the poems, their avoidance of ornate diction and rhetorical tropes, their discontinuities and ellipses, their metaphysical silences. Yet this poetry came to dominance under Mussolini as a defense against Fascism, a withdrawal from hopeless political action to record personal experiences and revelations, at once dramatic and transitory. At a time when the Fascist regime was encoding linguistic and cultural forms with collective ideologies, both totalitarian and nationalist, poetry might be seen as a practice of resistance through intricate works of self-expression.

Pozzi wrote most of her poems during the 1930s when the regime was tightening its hold through censorship and propaganda. The year of her death, 1938, was climactic: in May Hitler visited Italy amid speeches celebrating the Rome-Berlin Axis; in August the Fascists instituted racial laws that led Italian Jews into hiding or exile. Pozzi was shocked when her friends Paolo and Piero Treves chose to emigrate with their family that summer. Her suicide note links her "mortal desperation" partly to the "cruel oppression that is exerted upon our faded youth."

It was also during this decade that Mussolini actively pursued his imperialist aspirations, capitalizing on the Italian colonies that had already been established in Eritrea and Somalia. In December 1934 Ethiopian troops attacked an Italian unit, providing him with a rationale for invasion. At the end of January 1935, Pozzi wrote a poem entitled "Africa," a sequence of awe-struck images about the desert, its monumentality, its timelessness, its endless uniformity of color. The poem ends:

> o terra,
> cielo vento—
> libertà
> di sogni.
>
> o earth,
> sky wind—
> > dream
> > freedom.

Hermeticism transforms geopolitical spaces into images of private transcendence.

Nonetheless, Pozzi's poetry glances at a more critical attitude toward Italian nationalism and its consequences. At the beginning of October 1935, when a huge Italian force invaded Ethiopia, she wrote a poem entitled "Le donne" ("The women") where the image of patriotic women "a tricolori abbraciate" ("hugging the tricolor") is juxtaposed to the first war casualties.

For the most part, Pozzi's poems are frankly autobiographical, intimately connected to decisive moments in her life.

These moments began at age five, when her parents purchased an eighteenth-century villa in Pasturo, a small village in the mountains of northeastern Lombardy, the Valsassina area. Then at fifteen she developed a strong attachment to Antonio Maria Cervi, a classics professor at her secondary school, with whom she ultimately fell in love. Cervi, who was fourteen years older, responded in kind, but her parents forbade her to marry him. Their opposition stemmed, most likely, from the fact that as her teacher Cervi occupied a position of authority and trust that he violated with his romantic involvement. He posed a threat because he challenged their control over their daughter, who was their only child.

When the affair was discovered in 1928, Pozzi's father intervened to have Cervi transferred from Milan to a school in Rome. Then the parents tried to distract their daughter by sending her on trips to England and the south of Italy. The lovers continued to correspond and met secretly. Cervi traveled to London on one occasion. The correspondence indicates that the relationship lasted for several years but buckled under the weight of the parents' opposition. There was also a significant cultural difference: Cervi was a devout Catholic who felt uneasy about Pozzi's agnosticism, a result of her secular upbringing in the Milanese bourgeoisie. In 1933 she apparently ended the relationship, even if the letters persisted into the following year, recriminating, yet still loving.

Because Pozzi seems to have regarded her poems as a diary, she dated all of them and assigned locations to many, sites where the scenes she depicted had unfolded and where the poems were written. Many record her deeply felt experiences in the Lombard mountains, presenting finely observed evocations of psychological landscapes. Others represent key moments in her frustrated affair with Cervi: memories of rendezvous, passionate and affecting; utopian hopes for their future, including her obsessive desire to bear his son; bleak expressions of thwarted love. When, near the end of her life, she worked among the poor in the tenements of Milan, this experience too entered a poem whose title she took from a street name: "Via dei Cinquecento."

Pozzi wrote poetry that was at once personal and pastoral, that figured her complex emotional life in simple aspects of nature. This dimension of her work, revealed in a lyric expressiveness that ran counter to hard-edged hermeticism, is more suggestive of certain late-nineteenth-century trends: the *scapigliatura* (*scapigliato* means "disheveled"), a bohemian movement that resorted to heightened, Gothic depictions of love and beauty, and *crepuscolarismo* (*crepuscolo* means "twilight"), a loosely affiliated group that favored introspective, somewhat pessimistic musings on everyday events. Yet Pozzi's forms and themes can also be illuminated if Giovanni Pascoli is included among her diverse influences.

A classics professor jailed on several occasions for his socialist politics, Pascoli wrote poems about the Italian countryside that are at once Virgilian and suffused with his own melancholic experiences. Here is a brief poem entitled "Pianto" ("Weeping") from his collection *Myricae* (1891–1903), along with a free rendering that aims to give some sense of its prosodic effects:

> Più bello il fiore cui la pioggia estiva
> lascia una stilla dove il sol si frange;
> più bello il bacio che d'un raggio avviva
>   occhio che piange.

> More lovely is the flower where a summer shower
> distills a drop that bends the sun awry;
> more lovely is the kiss that brightens with bliss
>   a tearful eye.

As the poem suggests, Pascoli was a master of traditional stanzaic forms, metrically regular and rhymed, occasionally with a refrain. Their influence can perhaps be glimpsed in a poem like Pozzi's "Echi" ("Echoes"), where she used a repetitive, song-like structure to organize her jagged free verse.

Although Pascoli was not a modernist, he promoted what he called a "modernization of the poetic lexicon to renew Italian poetry." In practice this meant extracting subtle resonances from plain yet precise language. He also pursued a poetic experiment that was likely to be attractive to Pozzi: onomatopoeia, sound effects designed to mimic natural phenomena, like birdsong or thunder. He assigned poetry a metaphysical aim: to release the hidden music of things.

As Montale quickly saw, Pozzi's poetry is comparable to "canzonieri d'oggi," latter-day reinventions of Petrarch's sonnet sequence which aim to "give a full portrait of a 'person.'" Like numbered sonnets, her poems sketch the history of a love affair, and they evoke a voice that resonates with psychological nuances.

As in the Petrarchan tradition, furthermore, the theme of memory assumes considerable importance in Pozzi's work, particularly because of her severed relationship to Cervi. Her poems recall the beloved at significant moments in the past, sometimes detaching a physical detail and charging it with emotion, a smile or tone of voice, eyes or lips. Yet this fragmentation of the beloved never underwrites a subjective integrity in the poet-lover, who remains equally fragmented by desire. Verb tense and mood become crucial components here, useful in representing a future projection or a life in the subjunctive. In poems such as "Convegno" ("Rendezvous") and "Certezza" ("Certainty"), abrupt temporal shifts juxtapose an encounter that has yet to occur with memories that compensate for a present feeling of emptiness.

The psychological emphasis that Petrarchism is likely to bring to any poetry was revised by Pozzi's modernism. Like such poet-theorists as Eliot, she occasionally described poetic self-expression in biological terms. In 1933 she wrote to her friend, the poet Tullio Gadenz, that "because of an experience that burns through my entire life, because of an innate, irrevocable adherence to the most profound existence, I believe in poetry. And I live on poetry the way veins live on blood." Biology was her metaphor for a philosophical understanding of poetry that suggests Nietzsche and Heidegger and is sometimes couched in theological language. Poetry, Pozzi wrote to Gadenz, released the "divine flow" of life by "shattering" the "determinate forms" that "shackle" it. What received expression in poetry was transindividual, finally, a way of "*living* deeply" in language, an authentic existence.

Pozzi's modernist lyrics are not conversational but dramatic, not coherent but fractured. The voice she evokes is usually constructed out of rapid descriptions and analogies, and therefore it is always decentered by the landscape, the weather, a season, a time of day, a quality of light—as well as a wide range of events and emotions. Partly this technique reflects the excruciating sensitivity that characterized her mode of address to the world. In a diary entry from 1935, she described her "disorder" as the feeling that "everything for me is a wound through which my personality is on the brink of gushing, surrendering itself."

Yet she also knew that a disjunction exists between feeling and word, that self-expression in poetry is not so much achieved as complicated by the process of self-construction in language. Art is not life, she argued, but a compensation for frustrated desire. In another letter to Gadenz from 1933, Pozzi explained the "sublime task" of poetry:

> to take all the pain that rages over us and shatters our souls, and to soothe it, to transfigure it into the supreme calm of art, just as rivers flow into the blue vastness of the sea. Poetry is a catharsis of pain, as the immensity of death is the catharsis of life.

Here poetry is likened to death. It is a cultural practice wherein the desire to be free from pain is satisfied, offering a release from the forms that constrain life, creating a higher life that answers to, but is so different from, material realities.

For Pozzi, poetry was the place where her identity was hopelessly conflicted. In letters to Vittorio Sereni during 1935, she compares herself to Tonio Kröger, convinced more than ever of the "incompatibility of poetry and life." For Thomas Mann's character, "life" comes to mean marriage to a childhood sweetheart, a path that Kröger chose not to take because of his writing; for Pozzi, it means being "a real woman," a wife to a husband like her classmate, the philosopher Remo Cantoni, adapting to the "practical life" she so much resisted, "losing the most true and least banal part of myself." She imagines a grim fate in which she is neither wife nor poet: "Perhaps my destiny is truly to write beautiful books of fairy tales for children I will never have." Like Kröger, Pozzi entertains a writerly fascination with what he calls "the bliss of the ordinary," *den Wonnen der Gewöhnlichkeit*—in her case, not only marriage and motherhood, but the mountains in Lombardy, the land, its simple people. Yet she is unable to lead an ordinary life because of her interest in poetry. Pozzi, unlike Kröger (or Mann), understood this contradiction in the light of the social constrictions she faced as a woman.

Her divided feelings towards her poetry are most apparent in the ways that she revealed its existence. Of course Pozzi sent Cervi poems that she had dedicated to him; she even wrote an early poem about copying some for him "in a school notebook." Her letters and diary entries also indicate that she showed her poems to friends and classmates at the university, to the Treves brothers, Remo Cantoni, Enzo Paci. She made a particular effort to show her poems to poets whose work she admired: Tullio Gadenz and Vittorio Sereni. Sereni even read certain poems that remain unpublished today, and some of her phrases so impressed him that he echoed them in later poems of his own.

All the same, Pozzi's poetry had a very limited circulation. And she seems always to have treated it with extreme modesty. The title she had written on her notebooks was devoid of literary pretensions: it was simply "Parole" ("Words"). In "Copiatura" ("Copying"), dedicated to Cervi, she refers to her work as "le mie poesiucole," my poetic trifles. In a memoir published in 1941 Gadenz recalled the day when, "in making me read several of her most beautiful compositions, she presented them as the songs of an unknown poet."

With others, self-effacement metamorphosed into harsh self-criticism. In February 1935, after mentioning her poetry to her teacher Antonio Banfi, she wrote in her diary: "Why did I tell him that I write horrible verses?" She was very much aware of his doubts regarding hermetic poetry; in fact, she recapitulated them in the conclusion to her thesis on Flaubert, where she asserted that the discontinuous form typical of hermeticism led to an "intuitive arbitrariness," giving contemporary poetry "the character of an evasion and an internal retreat, no longer a comprehension and resolution of the complete life." After reading her poems, Paci advised her, "Write as little as possible," perhaps in agreement with Banfi's views. This response also precipitated a crisis of self-confidence. In her diary Pozzi asked herself:

> What authorizes me to attribute any importance whatsoever to an activity that until yesterday I considered not a duty, but a spiritual pleasure, not hard work, but a consolation? What right have I to think that I am somebody?

It seems significant that Pozzi's ambivalence toward her poetry was displayed in her interactions with men. Her poetic models, her teachers, her classmates were, with few exceptions, men. The most decisive figures in her life were men. She showed them her poetry but at the same time felt that it prevented her from being a proper wife, "a real woman," or even a good student, especially in their eyes.

It was in her poetry, however, that Pozzi gained a particular kind of control over her life. She took charge of its representation. She celebrated the pleasure and managed the pain of her relationships with men, including the male poets who influenced her. And she seems to have shared the greatest number of her poems with women who, she believed, could understand the psychological traumas it represented. In an intense letter to Cervi, one of her last to him, she made clear her feeling that only a woman could comprehend her unsatisfied desire to bear his child.

It is appropriate, then, that a woman who was one of her closest friends proved to be instrumental in preserving her poems. Pozzi made a habit of slipping manuscript versions into Lucia Bozzi's pockets, and not only did Bozzi save these loose sheets but she recopied other poems into her own set of notebooks. Pozzi's editors subsequently relied on these copies to restore the texts that her father had altered and to establish the definitive edition of her poetry.

The aesthetic that informed Pozzi's writing developed in the course of her brief life. Poetry was joined by prose, the lyrics by a historical novel, self-expression by social engagement. She worked on these projects during the same period and saw them as causing an unsettling shift in consciousness. Writing in 1934 to Tullio Gadenz, she notes, "While I was thinking of new problems whose existence I had hitherto ignored (society, politics, individualism and collectivism) I lost my true being, the tone and equilibrium of my personality: the reign of dreams and poetry collapsed." She concluded her thesis on Flaubert by suggesting that prose was an effective vehicle to "resolve the crisis of the incompatibility between art and life suffered by various Tonio Krögers, by the latest *poètes maudits.*"

Thus Pozzi began to draft chapters of a novel that explored class divisions in late-nineteenth-century Lombardy. Her letters to her maternal grandmother, Maria Cavagna Sangiuliani, reveal the nature and depth of her interest in this project. Pozzi's requests for information encompass chronologies, farming techniques, the local convent school, and the sort of sensory details that distinguish her poetry, "the color of the ponies you tamed, the smell of the dormitory rooms, the fabric that was used to make your aprons." Her imagination dwelt on the ordinary and turned political, leading her "towards more democratic constructions, towards the simple, elementary sense of the land and its poor people."

It might be argued that Pozzi's cushioned life in the bourgeoisie prevented her from developing the social consciousness that motivated her plan to write a historical novel. The emphasis on private experience in her poetry, the strong autobiographical tendency, seems to have further insulated her thinking, preempting "democratic constructions." Her poetry does in fact contain images of the working class and the poor. Yet a poem like "La disgrazia" ("Mishap"), where she depicts a dairy boy's injury, avoids any social representation to express compassion, even sentimentality; and in "Echi" ("Echoes"), a poem about women mowing, labor is submitted to the abstraction of poetic form. In other poems, interestingly, class relations obtrude on the aestheticized landscape. "Sera a settembre" ("September evening") accumulates several delicately atmospheric images that are finally disturbed by the lament of gypsies. "Cervino" is even more explicit: the Alpine mountain is likened to the "ribellione di massi" ("revolt of the masses"), a phrase in which the word "massi," referring to size or bulk, puns on the word "masse," referring to crowds or the common people.

Despite Pozzi's growing social consciousness, she never

stopped writing powerful poetry in the hermetic style. After presenting her thesis late in 1935, she produced roughly fifty more poems in the last three years of her life. And when her body was found in 1938, her hand was grasping a sheet of paper where she had copied Vittorio Sereni's poem "Diana," an affectionate invocation of the classical goddess moving through contemporary Milan. If Pozzi's approach to poetry remained deeply personal, did she see herself in this poem by an intimate friend? Was she aware that Sereni had addressed it to Maria Luisa Bonfanti, who was studying literature at the University of Milan and would soon become Sereni's wife? Was Pozzi's suicide immediately precipitated by another disappointment in love?

In 1955 the British publisher John Calder issued a bilingual selection of Pozzi's poems rendered into English by Nora Wydenbruck, a translator of Rilke. Wydenbruck presented them as a record of Pozzi's experiences with Lombardy, imbued with the sadness that led to her tragic end. A family friend contributed a memoir of the "late poetess."

Wydenbruck's interest was welcomed by the Pozzi family. In her preface she thanks the poet's father "for his kind and patient help in elucidating obscure passages." She translated the texts that he had edited: her version of "The skylark" reflects his deletion of the opening phrase, "After the kiss." She also tried to efface the modernist style of the poems by smoothing out the discontinuities. A reviewer for the *Times Literary Supplement* described her translation as "overscrupulous sometimes in its purpose of making the original as intelligible as possible."

Wydenbruck herself wrote that "English is perhaps the language best adapted to imitate the terseness and render the delicate overtones of Antonia's diction." But this observation seems to have had little effect on her translating. With the poem "Sole d'ottobre" ("October sun"), for instance, where Pozzi's Italian reads simply "bianca bellezza" ("white beauty") or "in quella [veste]" ("in that [clothing]"), Wydenbruck's English inflates and exoticizes: "white, dazzling splendour," "under his veils."

Against the backdrop of British and American poetic traditions, Antonia Pozzi conjures up suggestive resemblances, some more telling than others. Emily Dickinson and Sylvia Plath come readily to mind: the woman whose unsettling poetry is dubiously edited by friends and relatives is now a familiar figure in our literary history. The mark of a compelling translation, however, is its impact on the native literary traditions that it must use to rewrite the foreign work. Pozzi offered me an unusual opportunity to test the expressive possibilities of modernist poetry in English—and to make it a little less familiar.

Relying on recent editions of the Italian texts that return to her notebooks and manuscripts, I have tried to recreate precisely those features that Wydenbruck perceived in the poems. When I read the Italian, however, I heard the stripped-down classicism of H.D. and the angular but mellifluous rhythms of Lorine Niedecker, performances in modernist poetic idioms (imagism, objectivism) quite like *ermetismo*. I even recalled specific poems, like H.D.'s "Wine Bowl" (1931) or Niedecker's suite, "In Exchange for Haiku" (1959), which contains this piece:

> July—waxwings
> on the berries
> have dyed red
>   the dead
> branch

The sound effects that I have sought were not so much in the Italian as inspired by its abrupt musicality, now resonant with Anglo-American poetries.

Especially those written by women. My reading of the Italian texts was mindful that women have played a significant role in building modernist poetic traditions in English: H.D., Amy Lowell, Mina Loy, Lorine Niedecker seem most pertinent to Pozzi in form and theme. My translation affiliates her poetry with theirs in order to reproduce her hermetic style. Yet in establishing this connection the English supplies what she lacked in Italian: a tradition of modernist women poets.

My strategy has guided my choice of poems to translate. I wished to create a selection that respected the important autobiographical dimension of Pozzi's work, especially her relationship with Cervi, but without letting her life displace her interest in poetic form. I have therefore tended to include poems that better lend themselves to a modernist idiom. Very few overlap with the selection in Wydenbruck's version, where the poet's life takes precedence over her poetry.

A translation that draws on resemblances between the foreign poems and poetries in the translating language inevitably highlights differences—of tone and music, diction and syntax, theme and discourse. Pozzi's poetic lexicon includes words like "cuore" ("heart") and "anima" ("soul," "spirit"), which were not trite in her moment but have come to seem so today, especially in English. Ezra Pound referred to this problem in 1929 (the first year of Pozzi's poetic diary) when introducing his versions of the medieval poet Guido Cavalcanti. "Derivative convention and loose usage," he wrote, "have obscured the exact significance of such phrases as: 'The death of the heart,' and 'The departure of the soul.'"

Pound felt that in such cases of linguistic and cultural difference a translation experimentalism was warranted because "the modern audience must in some measure be made aware of the mental content of the older audience." And so he not only retained words like "heart" and "soul" but resorted to occasional archaisms, obsolete words and phrases, whereby his translations helped to situate the poems stylistically in the past.

I have found Pound's example useful, especially in signaling the trace in Pozzi's poems of a turn-of-the-century figure such as Giovanni Pascoli. Not only have I occasionally translated into archaic diction and syntax, but I have sometimes departed from the prosodic freedom of the Italian texts to create quasi-stanzaic structures and rhyme schemes, usually off-rhymes. These strategies might be seen as injecting a Pascolian note into an otherwise modernist style. Readers of contemporary American poetry might also be reminded of projects like Robert Creeley's *For Love* (1962), where modernist poems deeply indebted to William Carlos Williams's plain-language free verse are modeled on the rhyming stanzas of Elizabethan love lyrics.

Of course, no reader is likely to confuse the poetries that this translation puts into play. On the contrary, Pozzi's Lombard landscape, her personal dramas, her shattering experiences, her tragic death all ensure that any resemblance to poets living or dead is purely . . . uncanny.

Poems

"The Water's Fury," Breil 1933. Photograph by Antonia Pozzi.

Se le mie parole potessero
essere offerte a qualcuno
questa pagina
porterebbe il tuo nome.

If my words could be
                    an offering
          to someone
                    this page
would bear your name.

Giacere

Ora l'annientamento blando
di nuotare riversa,
col sole in viso
—il cervello penetrato di rosso
traverso le palpebre chiuse—.
Stasera, sopra il letto, nella stessa postura,
il candore trasognato
di bere,
con le pupille larghe,
l'anima bianca della notte.

Santa Margherita, 19 giugno 1929

Lying

Now the tranquil
                annihilation
        swimming
    on my back
sun in the face—brain
drowned in red
through tight lids—.
This evening in bed
                the same
position the dreamy
        bright pupils
dilated drink
the blanc
        soul
of night.

Innocenza

Sotto tanto sole
nella barca ristretta
il brivido
di sentire contro le mie ginocchia
la nudità pura d'un fanciullo
e l'ebbro strazio di covare nel sangue
quello ch'egli non sa.

Santa Margherita, 28 giugno 1929

Innocence

Sun flooding
the tight boat
        shudder
against my knees
of a boy's
            pure
        nudity
& the rapt
    agony
hatching in the blood
what he doesn't
know.

Ultimo crepuscolo

L'acqua gioca con gli scogli
sbavando
come un cavallo sudato
—due paranze ritornano
con le vele flosce—
Sola sul trampolino,
coi miei vaneggiamenti importuni,
ostento nel grigio
la mia maglia scarlatta:
ma—dentro—l'anima
illividisce
come la carne molle
di un bambino annegato.

Santa Margherita, 30 giugno 1929

Late twilight

Water plays in the reef
     drooling
like a sweaty horse—
two trawlers come
back with flaccid
       sails—solo
  on the diving
          board
with my importunate
      raving
  I show off
my scarlet
     jumper
in the grey light:
    but inside
  soul feels
      livid
like the soft flesh
of a drowned baby.

Copiatura

ad A.M.C.

Nel giallore temporalesco
le mie poesiucole
ricopiate su un quaderno di scuola
per te.
L'anima s'appiattisce
tra passato e presente
come un'avvinazzata corolla di papavero
—a ricordo d'un idillio di viaggio—
fra le pagine di una guida turistica.

Pasturo, 1 settembre 1929

Copying

In the stormy
                    yellow
          light
my poetic trifles
    recopied
                    for you
in a school notebook.
Spirit
      lying in wait
between past & present
like a drunk
                    poppy—
                    memory
of an idyllic journey—
in the pages
of a baedeker.

Presagio

Esita l'ultima luce
fra le dita congiunte dei pioppi—
l'ombra trema di freddo e d'attesa
dietro di noi
e lenta muove intorno le braccia
per farci più soli—

Cade l'ultima luce
sulle chiome dei tigli—
in cielo le dita dei pioppi
s'inanellano di stelle—

Qualcosa dal cielo discende
verso l'ombra che trema—
qualcosa passa
nella tenebra nostra
come un biancore—
forse qualcosa che ancora
non è—
forse qualcuno che sarà
domani—
forse una creatura
del nostro pianto—

Milano, 15 novembre 1930

Omen

The last light fades
on the poplars'
          joined fingers—
     shadow
shivers with cold &
               waiting
     behind us
slowly slips around its arms
          making us
more alone—

The last light falls
on the lindens'
                    tresses—
     in the sky
               the poplars'
               fingers
slip on starry rings—

Something drops
                    from above
towards the shivering shadow—
something cuts the dark
     a gleam—may be
something not yet—
someone who will be
                    tomorrow—
          a creature
          of our grief—

La disgrazia

È caduto il ragazzo
del lattivendolo, su per le scale:
un gran rimbombo
nella penombra fredda.
Gronda giù dalle rampe,
a larghe gocciole, il latte
delle bottiglie infrante,
commisto al sangue
delle mani ferite.
Quanto sangue, Signore,
in due povere mani di bambino!
Sulla sudicia pietra
del pianerottolo, ingrossano
pozze di latte cilestrino, opaco,
pozze di sangue rosso, abbacinante,
selvaggiamente libero,
selvaggiamente lieto.
Sopra una sedia dura
della nostra cucina,
bianco, ammollito, il piccolo
sembra ascoltare
il rodìo caldo
del suo sangue che fugge.
Fuori, per tutti i canali,
insiste
il rodìo freddo
della pioggia che cade.

3 maggio 1931

Mishap

The dairy boy
                fell
     up the stairs:
          a shattering
       roar
in cold twilight.
Pouring down
                    steps
     abrupt gushes
          milk
       from broken bottles,
mixed with blood,
his cut hands.
     God how bloody,
his poor childish hands.
On the grimy stone
                        landing
     spreading puddles
          milk
bluish, opaque—
                    & red
                    blood,
          dazzling,
     violently free,
     violently happy.
On a hard chair
in our kitchen,
                    pale,
          mollified
the little one listens
to the warm
                gnawing
of his escaping blood.
     Outside
in every ditch
the cold
          gnawing
of falling rain
     insists.

15

Nostalgia

C'è una finestra in mezzo alle nubi:
potresti affondare
nei cumuli rosa le braccia
e affacciarti
di là
nell'oro.
Chi non ti lascia?
Perché?
Di là c'è tua madre
—lo sai—
tua madre col volto proteso
che aspetta il tuo volto.

Kingston, 25 agosto 1931

Nostalgia

A window
   in the midst
      of cloud:
         you could
   thrust
your arms
into the pink
   cumulus
& look out
         beyond
         into the gold.
Who doesn't let you?
Why?
     Beyond
        lies your mother—
        you're sure—
   her face
leaning out
   awaiting
         yours.

Grido

Non avere un Dio
non avere una tomba
non avere nulla di fermo
ma solo cose vive che sfuggono—
essere senza ieri
essere senza domani
ed acciecarsi nel nulla—
—aiuto—
per la miseria
che non ha fine—

10 febbraio 1932

Scream

Don't
    have a god,
     no grave
   nothing
      fixed
only the living
    escape—being
without yesterday
     & tomorrow
  blinded
in the nothing—SOS—
    the sadness
    is endless—

Paura

Nuda come uno sterpo
nella piana notturna
con occhi di folle scavi l'ombra
per contare gli agguati.
Come un colchico lungo
con la tua corolla violacea di spettri
tremi
sotto il peso nero dei cieli.

Milano, 19 ottobre 1932

Fear

Naked
      as a branch
    at night
on the plain, eyes
            crazed
     you hollow
   shadow
      counting
the traps.
Like a tall crocus
    your purple
          corolla
    of ghosts
you shudder under
   the black
       weight
of the skies.

Sogno nel bosco

Sotto un abete
per tutto un giorno
dormire
e l'ultimo cielo veduto
sia in fondo all'intrico dei rami
lontano.

A sera
un capriolo
sbucando dal folto
disegni
di piccole orme
la neve
e all'alba
gli uccelli
impazziti
infiorino di canti il vento.

Io
sotto l'abete
in pace
come una cosa della terra,
come un ciuffo di eriche
arso dal gelo.

16 gennaio 1933

A dream in the forest

Perchance to sleep
        beneath a fir
  a whole day
spying the last sky
        behind
a network of branches
  faraway.

At dusk
      a goat
blasting a hole
   through a thicket
   might trace tracks
      in the snow
& at dawn
maddened
      birds sow
the wind
with song.

Me
in peace
      beneath a fir
like some thing
  of the earth
       a patch
  of heather
    singed
    by frost.

Scena unica

Vedi:
questo è il mio bambino
finto.

Gli ho fatto il vestitino
all'uncinetto
con la lana bianca.

Dice anche "mamma"—
sì—
se lo rovesci sopra il dorso.

Dammelo qui in braccio
per un pochino:
ecco,
hai sentito
come ha detto

"mamma"?

Questo è il mio bambino—
vedi—
il mio bambino
finto.

31 gennaio 1933

One act

Look: this is
    my fake
baby.

I knitted him
    a singlet
in white wool.

He says
        "mamma"—
    if I roll
him over.

Let me hold him
    a little bit:
d'you hear
how he said

"mamma"?

This is my baby—
            you see
    the resemblance—
my doll
baby.

Luce bianca

All'alba entrai
in un piccolo cimitero.

Fu in un paese lontano
ai piedi di una torre grigia
senza più voce alcuna
di campane—
mentre ancora la nebbia
inargentava
le querce oscure,
le siepi alte,
l'erica
viola—

Nel piccolo cimitero
le pietre
volte all'Oriente
come in un riso
bianco
parevano visi di ciechi
che allineati marciassero
incontro al sole.

1 febbraio 1933

White light

At dawn
       I entered a little
cemetery.

A remote village
   at the foot
of a grey tower
     the bells
soundless — mist
       still
      silvering
dark oaks,
tall hedges
    purple
  heather —

In a little
   cemetery
stones turned
towards the East
        as if
   in a blank laugh
 like blind
 faces lined
      up
& marching
against the sun.

Gli eucalipti

Alti gli eucalipti lungo l'argine
effusi al piede
in uno sgorgo acceso di papaveri—
Crepitano le foglie péndule
nel vento—
qualcuna cade
imbiancata
dalla calura—
lungo il canale profondo naviga—
piccola falce—
come la prima luna
nell'aria oscura—

16 maggio 1933

Eucalyptus trees

Tall along
        the bank
    flowing at the root
in a burning gush
        of poppies—
    Drooping leaves
rattle in the wind—
        one two
                drop
    heat-whitened—
then sail along the deep
    canal—little
                scythes—
            like
a crescent moon
    the air opaque—

Acqua alpina

Gioia di cantare come te, torrente;
gioia di ridere
sentendo nella bocca i denti
bianchi come il tuo greto;
gioia d'essere nata
soltanto in un mattino di sole
tra le viole
di un pascolo;
d'aver scordato la notte
ed il morso dei ghiacci.

(Breil) Pasturo, 12 agosto 1933

Alpine water

The sheer joy
           of singing
      like you,
    torrential;
of laughing & feeling
        the teeth in my mouth
white like your gravelly shore;
of being born
          alone
          one
sunlit morning
amidst violets
in the pasture;
forgetting
      night
      the bite
    of the ice.

Respiro

Abbandono notturno
sul masso
al limite della pineta
e il tuo strumento fanciullesco
lentamente
a dire
che una stella
due stelle
sono nate
dal grembo del nevaio
ed un'altra sprofonda
dove la roccia è nera—

ed un lume va solo
sul ciglio del ghiacciaio
più grande di una stella
più fioco—
forse la lampada di un pastore—
la lampada di un uomo vivo
sul monte—
colloquio intraducibile
del tuo strumento
col lume dell'uomo vivo—

ascesa inesorabile dell'anima
di là dal sonno—
di là dal nero informe
stupore delle cose—
abbandono notturno
sul masso
al limite della pineta—

(Breil) Pasturo, 13 agosto 1933

Breath

Nocturnal abandon
     on the rock mass
  at the line
  where the pine
forest ends
& your child-like
mouth organ
  slowly counting
       one star
       two stars
   born from the womb
of snow drift
    & one more
  sinks
where the rock is black—

a lamp goes solo
    on the lip
  of the glacier
  larger
than a star
    fainter—perhaps
a shepherd's torch—
or a man
  living
on the mountain—
  untranslatable
  conversation
between your instrument
    & the light
  of that living man—

soul's relentless
  ascent
  past sleep
past the black formless
     stupor
   of things—

nocturnal abandon
  on the rock mass
   at the line
   where the pine
  forest ends—

Cervino

Ribellione di massi—
Cervino—
volontà dilaniata.

Tu stai di contro alla notte
come un asceta assorto in preghiera.
Giungono a te le nuvole
cavalcando
su creste nere:
dalle regioni dell'ultima luce
portano doni di porpora e d'oro
al tuo grembo.
Tu affondi nei doni i ginocchi:
chiami le stelle
che t'inghirlàndino
nudo.

Cervino—
estasi dura—
vittoria
oltre l'informe strazio—
eroe sacro.

(Breil) Pasturo, 20 agosto 1933

Cervino

Revolt of the masses—
    lacerated
      will.

You stand against
      night
   ascetic
consumed in prayer.
Clouds reach
    you riding
over black peaks:
from the lands at the end
      of light
bearing gifts
         purple
        & gold
to your lap
your knees
plunge in them:
you summon stars
    to wreathe
      your nudity.

Cervino—
      stiff
    ecstasy—
   victory
beyond the formless
         torture—
   sacred hero.

L'allodola

Dopo il bacio—dall'ombra degli olmi
sulla strada uscivamo
per ritornare:
sorridevamo al domani
come bimbi tranquilli.
Le nostre mani
congiunte
componevano una tenace
conchiglia
che custodiva
la pace.
Ed io ero piana
quasi tu fossi un santo
che placa la vana
tempesta
e cammina sul lago.
Io ero un immenso
cielo d'estate
all'alba
su sconfinate
distese di grano.
Ed il mio cuore
una trillante allodola
che misurava
la serenità.

25 agosto 1933

The skylark

After the kiss: we left
  the elms
     shadow
on the street
   heading back
   smiling at
      tomorrow
like tranquil babies.
Our hand-holding
formed a tenacious
        shell
  sheltering peace.
And I was
     levelled
  as if you were
some holy man
who calms the vain
    tempest
& walks on the lake.
I was
     immense

summer   sky

       dawn
       on

    boundless
sweeps of wheat.
Heart
   a trilling
    skylark
weighing
the strains
  of serenity.

Amore dell'acqua

Dalla valle ch'è un lago
di sole—agitato dall'onda
delle campane—
fugge l'ombra
e si aduna
sotto un albero solo
dove il torrente
cade—

Tutta l'ombra e la frescura del mondo
si serrano intorno
alla fronte accaldata
del bimbo
che—sporto sul ciglio—
l'anima abbandonata
svincolare non sa
dalle argentee braccia
della cascata—

12 settembre 1933

Watery love

From the valley
                    a lake
        of sun — stirred
            by the wave
of bells — shade
                    flees
        then gathers
beneath a lone tree
        where the torrent
            drops —

All the world's
                    cool
            shadow
tightens around
the child's
                    hot brow —
hanging over
the edge — can't shake
        the abandoned soul
                    loose
from silvery
                    arms
        cascading —

Morte delle stelle

Montagne—angeli tristi
che nell'ora del crepuscolo
mute piangete
l'angelo delle stelle—scomparso
tra nuvole oscure—

arcane fioriture
stanotte
nei bàratri nasceranno—

oh—sia
nei fiori dei monti
il sepolcro
degli astri spenti—

13 settembre 1933

How stars die

Mountains—sad
    angels
in the twilight hour
      your mute
    weeping
for the starry
    angel—
        disappeared
in dark cloud—

tonight
arcane flora
    will bloom
in the chasms—

oh—might
    the tomb
  of stars
bereft of glitter
    be
      mountain
  flowers—

La vita sognata

Chi mi parla non sa
che io ho vissuto un'altra vita—
come chi dica
una fiaba
o una parabola santa.

Perché tu eri
la purità mia,
tu cui un'onda bianca
di tristezza cadeva sul volto
se ti chiamavo con labbra impure,
tu cui lacrime dolci
correvano nel profondo degli occhi
se guardavamo in alto—
e così ti parevo più bella.

O velo
tu—della mia giovinezza,
mia veste chiara,
verità svanita—
o nodo
lucente—di tutta una vita
che fu sognata—forse—

oh, per averti sognata,
mia vita cara,
benedico i giorni che restano—
il ramo morto di tutti i giorni che restano,
che servono
per piangere te.

25 settembre 1933

The dreamt life

No one
        who talks to me
    knows
I lived another life—
                    a fairy tale
    as the saying goes
            or holy parable.

Because you were
                my purity
                white
wave of sadness
        broke
        over your face
if my impure lips
            named
    you, sweet
tears streamed
in the depths
        of your eyes
if we looked above—
that's why I seemed
            more pretty
        to you.

Veil
    of my youth,
my bright dress,
            truth
gone up in smoke—
        shiny
    knot—a whole
            life
dreamt—maybe—

& having dreamt
        you, dear life, I bless
the days that remain—
                the dead
            branch
of all the remaining days
        that serve to weep you.

43

La gioia

Domandavo a occhi chiusi
—che cosa
sarà domani la Pupa?—

Così ti facevo ridire
in un sorriso le dolci parole
—la sposa,
la mamma—

Fiaba
del tempo d'amore—
profondo sorso—vita
compiuta—
gioia ferma nel cuore
come un coltello nel pane.

26 settembre 1933

The joy

I shut my eyes
then asked
      "what will
      Babydoll
      be tomorrow?"

I made you
      repeat
      sweet
words, smiling
  "wife,
     mamma"

Fairy tale
     love time—
deep sip—life
       over—
          joy
    heart-steady
like a bread
  knife.

Riflessi

Parole—vetri
che infedelmente
rispecchiate il mio cielo—

di voi pensai
dopo il tramonto
in una oscura strada
quando sui ciotoli una vetrata cadde
ed i frantumi a lungo
sparsero in terra lume—

26 settembre 1933

Glare

Words—glasswork
how unfaithfully
                    you mirror
          my sky—

I thought of you
after sunset
on a dark street
when a window pane
          hit
the cobblestones
     & splinters
slowly scattered
                    the bright
          ground—

In sogno

Silenzio—grotte
di bianco cristallo
scavo
alle fiabe—

sul pianto il cuore trascorre—
sul lago celeste
con occhi grandi—cigliati
di glicine—

28 settembre 1933

Dreamt

silence—caves
of white crystal
   I hollow
in fables—

heart
     skimming over
   tears—
blue lake
eyes agape—lashes
      of wisteria—

Mattino

A lungo dalla luna infranto
or ricompone il lago
la sua incolumità
cerulea.
Presso l'isola inferma un cipresso
trae dalle nebbie le bende
per le ferite nascoste:
tacito prega, votando
il nuovo giorno—al cielo.

1 ottobre 1933

Morning

Long shattered
by the moon
        the lake
        regains
    secure
    azure.
Near the infirm
         island
    a cypress
drags bandages
    from the mists
for hidden wounds:
silent it prays,
offering the new day—
        to the sky.

Non so

Io penso che il tuo modo di sorridere
è più dolce del sole
su questo vaso di fiori
già un poco
appassiti—

penso che forse è buono
che cadano da me
tutti gli alberi—

ch'io sia un piazzale bianco deserto
alla tua voce—che forse
disegna i viali
per il nuovo
giardino.

4 ottobre 1933

I don't know

I think your smile
                sweeter
    than the sun
on this vase of flowers
already a bit
                faded—

maybe it's good
every tree
                drops
before me—

& I'm an empty white
piazza
        to
your voice—maybe
sketching
            paths
in the new
    garden.

Sole d'ottobre

Felci grandi
e garofani selvaggi
sotto i castani —

mentre il vento scioglie
l'un dopo l'altro
i nodi rossi e biondi
alla veste di foglie
del sole —

e il sole in quella
brucia
della sua bianca
bellezza
come un fragile corpo
nudo —

20 ottobre 1933

October sun

Giant ferns
& wild pinks
beneath the chestnuts—

wind loosening
    each red
        & blonde
        knot
on the sun's
leafy
    gown—

the sun
    ablaze
        in it
his white
beauty
like a fragile
        nude—

La voce

Aveva voce in te
l'universo
delle cose mute,
la speranza
che sta senz'ali nei nidi,
che sta sotterra
non fiorita.

Aveva voce in te
il mistero
di tutto che presso una morte
vuol diventare vita,
il filo d'erba
sotto le putride foglie,
il primo riso del bimbo salvato
a fianco di un'agonia
in una corsia
d'ospedale.

Or quando cade dagli alti
rami notturni
dei campanili—un rintocco—
e in cuore affonda come
il frutto dentro il campo arato—

allora hai voce
tu in me—
con quella nota
ampia e sola
che dice i sogni sepolti
del mondo, l'oppressa
nostalgia della luce.

10 dicembre 1933

The voice

spoke in you
   the universe
of mute things,
hope that lies
    unfledged in nests
or underground
nipped in the bud.

The mystery
spoke in you
   that everything
      near death
      wants life,
blade of grass
beneath rotted leaves
    first laugh
of the newborn
         delivered
         in the ward
  from agony.

Now
when a final note
falls from the high night
    branches
of the bell towers
        & plunges
  deep into my heart
grain in a ploughed field—
then your voice
    speaks in me—
  the tone
  full & alone
talking of all the dreams
  buried in the world,
the oppressive
      nostalgia
  for light.

Pensiero

Avere due lunghe ali
d'ombra
e piegarle su questo tuo male;
essere ombra, pace
serale
intorno al tuo spento
sorriso.

maggio 1934

A thought

of having two
                    long
                         wings
      pure shadow
& folding
them over this
              your pain;
of *being*
          shadow
    evening
peace around
your wasted
smile.

Incredulità

Le stelle—le nubi esiliate
di là dal vento
chissà per quali
spazi ignoti camminano.

Ieri correvan ombre
sulle nevi del colle—
come dita leggere.

Occhi non miei
che la nebbia invade—

Breil, 3 agosto 1934

Incredulous

Stars—
          clouds
      exiled beyond
      by the wind—
what nameless space
      do they embrace?

Yesterday shadows
                  ran across
the snow in the pass—
                      like nimble
                  fingers.

Eyes
      that don't belong to me
wherein the fog
                  seeps—

Odor di verde

Odor di verde—
mia infanzia perduta—
quando m'inorgoglivo
dei miei ginocchi segnati—
strappavo inutilmente
i fiori, l'erba in riva ai sentieri,
poi li buttavo—
m'ingombran le mani—

odor di boschi d'agosto—al meriggio—
quando si rompono col viso acceso
le ragnatele—
guadando i ruscelli il sasso schizza
il piede affonda
penetra il gelo fin dentro i polsi—
il sole, il sole
sul collo nudo—
la luce che imbiondisce i capelli—

odor di terra,
mia infanzia perduta.

Pasturo, agosto 1934

Green scent—

my lost childhood—
when I beamed about
        my bruised knees
        & uselessly
    ripped out
flowers, the grass at the edge of paths
        then threw them away—
my hands encumbered—

smell of forests
                in August—
        noon—
when face flushed
cobwebs break
& fording brooks
                stone skips
                foot sinks
the chill seeps as deep as the pulse—

        sun   sun

on my bare neck—
the light that lightens hair—

smell of earth,
my lost childhood.

Annotta

Il colore dei monti dice
il passare del tempo—
Ed è sera
quando le rocce svestono
il loro umano riso
di fiamma
e s'esiliano le cime
oltre il crepuscolo.
Allora muti—dal fondo
delle valli—crescon gli abeti,
le gigantesche foreste nere
a sommergere il giorno:
laghi d'azzurro invadono la neve,
mentre la notte ingoia
laggiù—le strade
e lenta scende la terra
nel buio.

San Martino, 7 gennaio 1935

Darkening

mountain
      color tells
  the lapse
of time—
at dusk
  rocks
     strip away
     their flaming
  human laugh
& the peaks
are exiled
      past
  the gloaming.
Then—from the depths
  of valleys—fir trees
     rise mute, huge
black woods submerge
     day: blue lake
  laps the snow,
as night swallows
     roads down below
  & earth
descends slowly
  into darkness.

Echi

Echi di canti vanno
sui pascoli alti,
treccie di falciatrici splendono
nel cielo.

Da lontani orizzonti viene il vento
e scrive parole segrete
su l'erba:
le rimormorano i fiori
tremando nelle lievi
corolle.

Echi di canti vanno
sui pascoli alti,
treccie di falciatrici splendono
nel cielo.

26 gennaio 1935

Echoes

Songs
  echo
over high
 pastures,
 mowers'
braids
shine in the sky.

From remote horizons
  wind arrives
  & writes
secret words
in the grass:
    flowers
    murmur
  them anew,
shuddering soft
 corollas.

Songs
  echo
over high
 pastures,
 mowers'
braids
shine in the sky.

Gelo

Brinato è il campo, dove tra le spighe
frusciò la mia veste leggera.

Ora dove tu sei
ravvia l'inverno
chiome di ghiaccio alle fontane:
il vento,
per le bianche cattedrali
delle foreste—ànima rotte querele
d'organo, dentro i rami.

Ora sepolti arpeggi
corron sul fondo
dei laghi: contro mute
gelide sponde muoiono,
infrangendosi.

28 gennaio 1935

Cold

Frost in the field
  where my thin frock
          rustled
amidst the grain.

Now where you are
  winter pins back
      the fountains'
frozen locks:
wind in the white
        cathedrals
  of the woods—quickens
the shattered organ
laments in the branches.

Now buried arpeggios
              slide
      across the bottom
of the lake: against mute
    icy shores
  they dash,
        dying.

Abbandono

Tronco reciso di betulla
giaci
in un solco:
a rosse onde declina
il tramonto pei cieli.

E sopra te le nubi
sandali d'oro calzano nel vento
per raggiungere
i fiumi.

Tu stai—bambino desto
nella tua culla
di terra:
mentre a un acceso volgere di mondi
con bianchi occhi s'incanta
la tua immobilità.

16 febbraio 1935

Forsaking

Hacked
   birch trunk
      you lie
in a furrow:
sun sets
   red waves
through the sky.

Above you
      clouds
      are shod
in the wind
with golden sandals
   to reach
the rivers.

You stay—
      my boy
wide awake in your crib
        of earth:
your stillness conjures
  a white-eyed spell
with the burning
     turning
  of worlds.

Stanchezza

Svenata di sogni
ti desti:
ti è pallida coltre
il cielo mattinale.

Come a un mortale
pericolo scampata,
con gesto umile—i gridi
delle campane scosti:

debolmente,
preghi nel poco sole
un silenzio.

17 febbraio 1935

Exhaustion

You lie
      awake
   bled
by dreams:
morning sky
         your pale
    blanket.

Like a lethal
      peril
         escaped
   with a humble
gesture—you distance
   screaming
      bells:

feebly praying
   in faint sunlight
for silence.

Fiabe

Vai a un reame di vento,
cauta rechi
sul capo una ghirlanda
di primule.

Sugli alberi le donne
con i capelli verdi,
nelle cascate i nani
che sanno il destino—

i pallidi guerrieri fra le barance,
le fanciulle che muoiono
per desiderio di sole—

e le capanne abbandonate
fra le miosotidi,
le pianure
d'asfodeli in cima alle rocce—

porte che si spalancano
su tesori sepolti,
arcobaleni che giacciono
infranti nei laghi—

Sali per la morena azzurra,
tra filari di guglie grigie:
porti sulle spalle
un bambino
addormentato.

18 febbraio 1935

Fairy tales

You trek to a realm
                         of wind,
              warily bearing
a garland of primrose
    on your head.

Women with green
                              tresses
         in trees,
dwarves in waterfalls
    who know destiny —

pale knights
              loitering
         amongst the pines,
young girls
              dying
    for want of sun —

& cabins
         abandoned
       amidst forget-me-nots,
fields of asphodel
    atop the peaks —

doors open wide
    on buried
treasure,
              rainbows lie
    shattered
    in lakes —

You climb the blue
                         moraine,
    between rows of grey spires:
borne on your back
         a baby
         asleep.

Dopo la tormenta

A mezza notte
col vento
una folata di stelle
s'abbatteva ai vetri.

Fino all'alba
velieri argentei di brume
in laghi d'ombra
percorrevano i prati.

Poi la luce
lenta riallacciava sulla fronte
del cielo
la corona delle montagne:

che si scopriva nel sole,
candida
di fresca neve—armoniosa
come un arco
di fiori.

18 febbraio 1935

After the snowstorm

Midnight
            wind
      a gust
of stars
            smashed
the windows.

Till dawn
            mist-silvered
      sail boats
in shadowy lakes
            traversed
the fields.

Then slowly
            light
      lays
the mountain's
      crown
on the sky's
      brow:

sun-found
            bright
      with fresh
snow—harmonious
like an arch
            of flowers.

Voli

Pioggia pesante di uccelli
su l'albero nudo:
così leggermente vibrando
di foglie vive
si veste.

Ma scatta in un frullo
lo stormo,
l'azzurro Febbraio
con la sera
sta sui rami.

È gracile il mio corpo,
spoglio ai voli
dell'ombra.

19 febbraio 1935

Flights

A heavy downpour
                        birds
            on a naked tree:
                        lightly
        quivering
        clothed
in living leaf.

But the flock
                scats
            in a flap, blue
        February
                hangs
on branches
with dusk.

My body is
                delicate,
                stripped
        in flights
            of shadow.

Smarrimento

Novembre
non è tornato:
ma i passeri
a mezzo giorno gridano
sugli alberi bagnati
come fosse per venir sera.

Qualcuno si è scordato
di rialzare i pesi
dell'orologio:
l'uccellino dice cucù
due volte soltanto,
poi resta sulla porticina
a guardare
il pendolo che a piccole scosse
si ferma.

Adesso
non so più
le ore.

21 febbraio 1935

Swoon

November didn't
return:
    but at noon
       the sparrows
       cry
on the soaked branches
as if night
       were about
       to fall.

Somebody forgot
       to fix
       the weights
in the clock:
the bird says
       cuckoo
just twice
    then stops on its porch
           to watch
the pendulum
       jerks
       to a halt.

Now
I can't tell
time.

Don Chisciotte

I

Sulla città
silenzi improvvisi.

Varchi
con un sorriso indefinibile
i confini:
sai le spine di tutte le siepi.

E vai,
oltre i fiati caldi degli uomini,
il sonno dopo gli amori,
l'affanno e la prigionia.

Su la petraia che è azzurra
come le corolle del lino,
liberata
canti correndo:

ma chiudi gli occhi
se in fondo al cielo
le ali bianche dei mulini
si dilacerano
al vento.

21 febbraio 1935

Don Quixote

I

A sudden silence
                    drops
          over the city.

You cross
          limits
     with an indefinable
                    smile:
you know the thorns
     in every hedge.

You go beyond
     the warm breathing
     of men, sleeping
after love,
               anguish
          & prison.

Woman set free
in song you dash
                    over rubble
               blue
          like linen
                    petals:

but you close
               your eyes
               at the sky's
          edge
if a gale
          shreds
the white wings
of the windmills.

II

Fioche
dalla terra brulla
ti giungono
grida atterrite:

mentre seguita
su l'ala immensa
a rotare
la tua crocefissione.

22 febbraio 1935

II

Terrified screams
from the naked
   earth
      reach
you faint:

as the huge
        whirling
      wing
    prolongs
your crucifixion.

Infanzia

Il mare
alle finestre
cadeva.
Onde verdi infrante
tinnivano sui vetri.
Era antica
la casa.
A piedi scalzi
tu correvi gli scogli:
ti tuffavi
per rubare le vongole gettate
dai pescatori.
A mezzogiorno
dal balcone del palazzo
una campana chiamava a riva
la tua gioia assolata
di bambino.

3 marzo 1935

Childhood

The sea heaved
    in the windows.
Shattered
green waves
        tinkling
  the panes.
The ancient
house.
Barefoot
you scoured reefs
& dove
     to filch clams
tossed by fishermen.
At noon
from the balcony
of the palazzo
  a bell
summoned ashore
your sunny
      boy's
      joy.

Pianure a maggio

In lucidi specchi
tra volti di nuvole bianche
si celano i grani
del riso.

Traspaiono strade
nel gracile bosco,
dai greti si porgono
al fiume.

Sugli alti viadotti
barcollano andando
lenti i carri
dell'erba recisa.

2 maggio 1935

Mayfields

In bright mirrors
amidst faces
  of white
        cloud
grains of rice
    hide.

  Roads shine
in the delicate wood.
  From the banks
they extend
     their offer
     to the river.

  Tottering
      on high
   viaducts
  carts
of mown grass
    go
    slow.

La notte inquieta

Dissepolte foglie
nei viali c'inseguirono, stridendo.
Rami
dai cancelli protesero
le loro ombre oscillanti
sull'asfalto.

Muti a sbocchi di strade
immobili fanali guardano
luci
a scroscio fuggenti,
tra rotaia e ruota
una scintilla verde che scocca.

Le case vogliono
pause di sonno
a occhi chiusi nel tremante silenzio:

ma passi
ancora
nascono agli svolti,

l'alba come una foglia
dissepolta c'insegue.

4 maggio 1935

Restless night

Leaves
          disinterred
     in paths
chased us down,
     screaming
branches reached
from gates
     their swaying
silhouettes crossed
          asphalt.

Mute at the exits
to the streets
immobile lamps
               sight
               lights
fleeing headlong,
between rail & wheel
          a green
     spark
flares out.

The houses desire
     breaks
          sleep
     shut-eyed
in the quivering
     silence:

but steps
          return
     to life
on the corners,

     dawn
          disinterred
like a leaf
chasing us down.

Creatura

Si faceva tua carne
il respiro
nel chiamarti a nome.

Per immense foreste camminammo:
i muschi
racchiudevano l'orma del tuo piede.

Foglie di quercia
ai capelli
furono piccole mani
alate di sole.

Ma a riva d'invernali fiumi
c'è sconosciuta
quest'alba:

la voce varca grigie onde
senz'echi,
gli aliti in nebbia rappresi e dissolti
ci consumano gli orli del tuo viso.

5 maggio 1935

Little one

    Breathing
        to name you
        became
your flesh.

    We stroll
        immense forests:
        moss moulds
your footprint.

    Oak leaves
in our hair
        tiny hands
    winged
        with sun.

    But on
wintry river banks
        this dawn is
    unknown:

    a voice crosses
grey waves
        echoless,
    misty
breath congealed
& dissipated
        eats the edges
    of your face.

Assenza

Il tuo volto cercai
dietro i cancelli.

Ma s'ancorava in golfo di silenzi
la casa,
s'afflosciavano le tende
tra i loggiati deserti,
morte vele.

Al largo,
a sbocchi d'irreali monti
fuggiva il lago,
onde verdi e grigie
su scale ritraendosi
di pietra.

Lenta vagò,
sotto l'assorto cielo,
la barca vasta e pallida:
vedemmo
in rosso cerchio crescere alla riva
le azalee, cespi muti.

Monate, 5 maggio 1935

Absence

I sought your face
behind gates.

But the house
was anchored
in a gulf
          of silences
curtains fell
            limp
between empty arcades,
      dead sails.

Offshore
the lake
        fled
    debouched
from unreal mountains,
grey-green waves
on stairs
          withdrawing
    from stone.

In a slow drift
beneath the rapt
                  sky,
        the boat
        vast
    & pale:
              we eyed
the red circle growing
on the shore
                azaleas,
      mute clusters.

Esclusi

Gioco di passi
a specchio dell'attesa
s'avvicenda negli occhi aperti e ciechi.

Lontano
ti relegano in penombra
le stanze mute ch'io non so,
mali — forse —
invisibili ti toccano.

A bordo della strada, coi ligustri
lenta divengo
un'inutile pianta:

non diamo ombre
nel giorno senza sole
a questi sassi intorno, volti spenti.

via Caradosso, 7 maggio 1935

Exclusions

Footfall plays
           in the mirror
      of wait
      alternates
in eyes
      agape
  & blind.

Faraway
      mute
      rooms
   I don't know
banish you
  to shadow,
invisible ills
may befall you.

Curbed
beside the privets
   I slowly turn
to useless
      bush:

on sunless days
          we cast
   no shadow
upon these dull-faced
     stones.

Fuga

Gracili volti porgono i narcisi
alla ventata.

Mani di bimbi:
e siepi
improvvise s'aggrappano ai cancelli.

Il respiro si strugge
alla mia corsa:

sguardi
alle cose gettati
—vani ponti—
mi divora l'abisso fragoroso.

10 maggio 1935

Escape

The narcissus leans
                        a fresh face
            into the breeze.

Children's hands:
                        abrupt
                        hedges
        grasp at gates.

Breath-blown
in my run:

glimpses
            of things
            rubbished—useless
        bridges—deafening
                        abyss
            devouring me.

Altura

La glicine sfiorì
lentamente
su noi.

E l'ultimo battello
attraversava il lago in fondo ai monti.

Petali viola
mi raccoglievi in grembo
a sera:
quando batté il cancello
e fu oscura
la via al ritorno.

11 maggio 1935

The heights

Wisteria bloomed
                    slowly
         over us.

The last boat
              crossed the lake
     at the foot of the mountains.

At dusk
         I gathered
      purple petals
in my apron:
when the gate banged
     the way back
                    plunged
         into darkness.

Intemperie

In rete d'acque
m'è rinato
il convento dell'infanzia.

Dove sei,
bianca scala?
                    Ti scendevo
tra le robinie
e non aveva fosse
la terra.

Ora in lontani viali
un compagno barcolla,
trasportando un morto:
gli cadono sul viso
le palpebre come spente viole.

Dove sei
scala bianca?
                    M'è sfuggito
un grido: manca il suolo.

Vampe d'incenso
per la via
non danno più riparo
a questa pioggia.

23 maggio 1935

Inclemency

In a watery net
my childhood
        convent
    flourished anew.

Where are you,
white stair?
        I descended you
amidst the locust trees
& the earth
        was free
    of depressions.

Now on remote paths
        a mate totters
    bearing a corse:
eyelids lowered
like spent
        violets.

Where are you
white
    stair?
        A scream
escaped me: the ground—
        she's gone.

Blasts
    of incense
    on the way
give no shelter
in this downpour.

Tempo

I

Mentre tu dormi
le stagioni passano
sulla montagna.

La neve in alto
struggendosi dà vita
al vento:
dietro la casa il prato parla,
la luce
beve orme di pioggia sui sentieri.

Mentre tu dormi
anni di sole passano
fra le cime dei làrici
e le nubi.

28 maggio 1935

Time

I

Whilst you sleep
　　　　seasons
　　　pass
over the mountain.

On high
　　　　snow
　　　　　in throes
gives birth
　　　to gales:
behind the house
　　　　　meadow
speaks, light
　　　drinks
　　　　　traces
　　　　　of rain
on the paths.

Whilst you sleep
　　　years
　　　　　of sun
　　　　stream
through the peaks
of larch trees
　　　& clouds.

II

Io posso cogliere i mughetti
mentre tu dormi
perché so dove crescono.
E la mia vera casa
con le sue porte e le sue pietre
sia lontana,
né io più la ritrovi,
ma vada errando
pei boschi
eternamente—
mentre tu dormi
ed i mughetti crescono
senza tregua.

28 maggio 1935

II

I can gather lilies
whilst you sleep
                    for I know
                    where they grow.
May my true house
          its doors, its stones
    be so faraway
    that I never lay
eyes on it again
wandering
                forests
                forever—
whilst you sleep
& lilies grow
        with no
respite.

Convegno

Nell'aria della stanza
non te
guardo
ma già il ricordo del tuo viso
come mi nascerà
nel vuoto
ed i tuoi occhi
come si fermarono
ora—in lontani istanti—
sul mio volto.

29 maggio 1935

Rendezvous

In the air
        of the room
        not you
do I regard
        just
        memory
   of your visage
as it will rise
        inside
           my void
& your eyes
as they focused
           now—
        in distant
        instants—
on my face.

Ora sospesa

Le case dove ogni gesto
dice un'attesa
che non si compie mai.

Il fuoco acceso nel camino
per sciogliere la nube del respiro
e in ogni cuore l'alba
di domani—col sole.

Tu—verso sera—farfalla
con le ali chiuse
tra due steli paventi
la pioggia.

30 maggio 1935

Suspense

Houses
where every move
  bespeaks
       a wait
that is never
     consummated.

Fire ablaze
in the hearth
   dissipating the haze
        of breath
& in every heart
tomorrow
    dawns—with the sun.

You—at dusk—
       close-winged
    butterfly
astride two stalks
    afraid
    of rain.

Dopo

Quando la tua voce
avrà lasciato la mia casa

rintorneranno di là dal muro
parole rauche di vecchi
a nominare nell'oscurità
invisibili monti.

Udirò greggi
traversare la notte:

il vento—curvo
sul letto dei torrenti—
scaverà
incolmabili valli nel silenzio.

2 giugno 1935

After

When your voice
      leaves
   my house

the old men's
    raucous talk
     will come back
over the wall
naming mountains
      invisible
  in the dark.

I shall hear
    herds
      crossing
  night:

wind—bowed over
   torrential
     beds—
hollowing out
    bottomless
   valleys
in silence.

Grillo

(Ohimé ch'io son tradita . . .)

Appaio e rompo
un canto di bambina
al ruscello.

Farfalle bianche
danzando
traversano il silenzio sull'acqua.

Ma dietro me rinasce
(. . . tradita nell'amor!):

grillo che si rintana
udendo passi
tra l'erba

e tosto al sole
risbuca, versa in trillo
il fugace
sgomento.

25 giugno 1935

Cricket

(Oh no I'm
       betrayed . . .)

I turn up
     & interrupt
  a girl's song
at the brook.

Dancing
     white
     butterflies
  traverse
silence
on the water.

But at my remove
it revives
(. . . betrayed
      in love!):

cricket
   holes up
detecting a step
in the grass

but darts back
into sunlight
     to chirp
his fleeting
dismay.

La vita

Alle soglie d'autunno
in un tramonto
muto

scopri l'onda del tempo
e la tua resa
segreta

come di ramo in ramo
leggero
un cadere d'uccelli
cui le ali non reggono più.

18 agosto 1935

Living

at the threshold
        of autumn
   in a mute
   sunset

you bare
the surge
   of time
  your secret
surrender

like birds falling
       lightly
  branch to branch
their wings
   no longer
   parted.

Precoce autunno

La nebbia è d'argento, cancella
le ombre dei pini:
sono più grandi i giardini
nell'alba.

Al pioppo una foglia è ingiallita,
un ramo è morto al castano
sul monte.

Spaventi che non sanno se stessi
dormendo nell'aria celeste:
questa fine che torna ogni anno,
che è nuova ogni anno.

Come l'ultimo albero del bosco,
l'ultimo uomo ha contato le morti:
pur la sua morte lo coglie
ancora stupito.

18 agosto 1935

An early fall

The fog is silvery,
                    erasing
        the shadows
of pine trees: gardens
                    enlarge
        at dawn.

Yellowed poplar leaf,
        withered branch
on the mountain chestnut.

Worry they don't know
if they're asleep
        in the blue air:
the end that comes back
        every year
                    anew.

Like the last tree in the wood,
        the last man reckoned
                    the dead:
he'll still be caught by surprise
            when he dies.

Leggenda

Mi portò il mio cavallo
tra le foglie
con soffice volo.

Calda vita nel vento
il suo respiro,
i molli occhi
fra colori d'autunno:
era oro nel sole il suo mantello.

Le pietre si scostavano
sui monti
al tocco degli zoccoli d'argento . . .

20 agosto 1935

Legend

My horse
        bore me
        through leaves
    a soft
    flight.

Living warmth
                in the wind
his breathing,
    tender eyes
            autumnal
            colored
his coat
    gold in the sun.

Stones shifted
in the mountains
            at the touch
    of his silver
                hooves . . .

Sul ciglio

Erbe intrise di guazza,
un fioco sole
tra nebbie, su dorsi di agnelli.

E a fianco il baratro:

spaventosa roccia,
a grembi di ghiaia sprofonda
livida.

Nascono le nuvole a mezza rupe
lente annodandosi,
mentre assorto traspare

il volto della terra nel vuoto.

Grigna, 22 agosto 1935

On the edge

Dew-sodden grass,
a weak hazy sun
            on the backs
    of lambs.

Flanked
            by chasm:

        terrible rock
                    drops
    straight into the lap
                of livid
                gravel.

Clouds rise
                slow
            & tangled
    halfway up the cliff,
as the face
                of the earth
        shines through

                absorbed
        in the void.

Ottobre

È crollo di morta stagione
quest'acqua notturna sui ciotoli.

Lànguono
fuochi di carbonai sulla montagna
e gela
nella fontana un fioco lume.

L'alba vedrà
l'ultima mandria divallare
coi cani, coi cavalli,
in poca polvere
dietro un dosso scomporsi.

Pasturo, 30 settembre 1935

October

This nocturne
            liquid
        over pebbles
collapse
of a dead season.

Languorous
            coal fires
        on the mountain
& a weak gleam
    freezes
            in the stream.

Dawn eyes
            the last
        flocks
descending
dogs, horses
a faint dust
over the ridge
        discomposed.

Le donne

In urlo di sirene
una squadriglia
fiammante spezza il cielo.

Rotte tra case affondano
le campane.

S'affacciano le donne
a tricolori abbracciate;
gridan coraggio
nel vento
i loro biondi capelli.

Poi,
occhi si chinano spenti.

Nella sera
guardan laggiù il primo morto
disteso sotto le stelle.

3 ottobre 1935

The women

Sirens
       shriek
& a blazing
squadron
         cleaves
the sky.

Cracked
       bells sink
   between houses.

The women
        lean
  out the windows
hugging the tricolor;
their blonde hair
            screams
      coraggio
in the wind.

Then, eyes
      lower
      burnt
      out.

In the evening
they look down
   at the first
         dead
         laid out
beneath the stars.

Sgelo

Ora la vuota strada
ci sospende
ai suoi lumi:

per aeree tombe portati,

mentre fuggono
acque lontane in basso
le parole.

E già domani
ad uno sbocco giungeremo:
sgelo
cáuto senza schianti,
la neve.

Lenta scendendo
ritroverò il tepore del mio volto:

quando
il suolo lieve mi fiorirà
la grazia
delle tue labbra.

18 dicembre 1935

Thaw

Now the voided
             road
      hangs us
from its lamps:

borne through airy tombs,

while words avoid
             remote
      waters
down below.

Tomorrow
we'll reach an outflow:
   melting
          cautious
  no cracks,
      snow.

Easing
     down my face
  regains
its warmth:

when
the soft soil blossoms
           in me
    the grace
of your lips.

Notturno

Lene splendore
di stelle
in vetta alle bandiere:

il vento
piega l'erba sulla fronte dei morti.

Da sùbite fronde si leva
l'uccello nerazzurro:

e cade
il remeggio del volo
grevemente
sul notturno monotono cuore.

18 dicembre 1935

Nocturne

Soft brilliance
of stars
  atop
banners:

wind folds
grass
  on the brow
of the dead.

A blueblack bird
takes wing
  from quickened
leaves

  & sinks
its beating
        flight
in a one-note
  heart
      at night.

Spazioso autunno

Or che i violini
hanno cessato di suonare

ed una foglia volteggiando
sfiora
il braccio bianco di Venere
in fondo al viale

andiamo per la brughiera
a veder nascere le stelle:

sono i visi delle ginestre morte.

Ora infuriano i cavalli nella stalla:
ma vagano lassù
con le nubi
le ombre delle lor lunghe criniere
rosse.

Inseguiamo fitte orme di zoccoli.

Ed è pieno di ali e di chiome
invisibili
quest'aperto campo notturno.

23 dicembre 1935

Capacious fall

Now the violins
             have ceased

& a turning
             leaf
         grazes
     the white arm
                 of Venus
at the foot of the path

we light out
     over the moor
to watch the stars
come out:

faces
of faded
         broom.

Now horses
             rage
in the stable:
but up above
                 the shadows
     of their long red
         manes
drift with clouds.

We follow
             close
         hoofprints.

Nightfall
         fills
this open field
with invisible
     wings
         & tresses.

Commiato

Si levarono alate di tormenta
le crode
sul gran volo della slitta:

poi declinò
con l'ombra del cavallo
il sole rosso
su dorsi di abeti.
Allora
accordi tenui di chitarra,
cori sommessi infranti, oltre le creste
corsero col tramonto
sul deserto
tinnulo trotto.

A sera
l'ultima mano rosea —
una pietra —
alta accennava
salutando:
e pallida
nell'aria viola pregava le stelle.

Lentamente
i fiumi a notte
mi portavano via.

Misurina, 11 gennaio 1936

Envoi

The crags rose
                winged
           with snow squalls
on the sleigh's
great flight:

& the red sun sank
      in a horse's shadow
on the backs
of fir trees.
Then faint
guitar chords,
           choruses
    soft, broken
beyond the peaks
raced with the sunset
over the hollow
    tinkling canter.

At evening
the last pink hand—
               a stone—
was beckoning above
      saluting:
           & pale
        in the violet air
prayed to the stars.

Slowly in the night
the rivers
were washing me
away.

Salita

Questa tua mano sulla roccia
fiorisce:
non abbiamo paura del silenzio.

Immenso grembo
la valle spegne l'ansia
di lontane valanghe,
fumo lieve
sulle pareti nere.

Si accendon le tue dita sulla pietra
alte afferrando
orli di cielo bianco:
non abbiamo paura del deserto.

Andiamo verso il Sorapis:
così soli
verso l'aperto
altare di cristallo.

Misurina, 11 gennaio 1936

Ascent

Your hand
        blooms
    on rock:
we weren't scared
   of silence.

Immense womb
the valley
     erases
dread of remote
avalanches—
        trace
   of smoke
on the black surface.

Your fingers
       alight
    on stone
grasping high
at the hem
     of white
   sky:
we weren't scared
   of wilderness.

Heading for
      Sorapis:
    alone
  like this
towards the open
        crystal
    altar.

Rifugio

I

Mentre di fuori il sole sgela
pelli di foca
ai cardini dell'uscio

scostate queste tazze di vin caldo
e il pane sbriciolato,
fate posto:
ora voglio dormire.

Se ridi
e scuoti il ciuffo del mio berretto rosso
come a un bambino insonnolito,
io cado
in golfi oscuri e caldi
di sogno.

Ma perché
una canzone marinaresca
fra strapiombi neri?

Shelter

I

Outside
      sun thaws
    seal-skin
on the door's hinges

as you clear away
    these cups of warm wine
    & crumbled bread,
you make room:
          now
      I'm ready to sleep.

If you laugh
      & shake
   the tassle
on my red beret
like a drowsy
        baby, I sink
   into gulfs
       dark
   & warm
with dream.

But why
   a sea
   chantey
amidst the black cliffs?

II

Dimmi che non possiamo
andare oltre:
questa pista finisce alla forcella,
alta e intatta è la neve
sul versante
dell'ombra.

Qui crediamo
eterna luce sovra campi splendenti:
potrà mai
venir sera ai nostri vetri
d'argento?

III

Noi,
quando grigie fascie di tormenta
strapperanno da terra
il nostro rosso
nido di pietra,
guarderemo nudi—
come da un celeste
Walhalla—
i laghi spenti in fondo ai pini,
le fioche
lampade erranti dei pastori.

19 gennaio 1936

II

Tell me we can't
               go farther:
         this track
         ends at the fork,
      the snow
               is deep
               & intact
on the other side
of the shadow.

Here we believe
eternal light
               above
      shining fields:
will night
ever fall
               on our silvery
      windows?

III

When grey bands
               of snow squall
      uproot
our red stone
                  nest
      naked we'll gaze—
as from a sky blue
               Valhalla—at empty
      lakes beneath pines
& the shepherds'
               dim wandering
      lamps.

Periferia

Lampi di brace nella sera:
e stridono
due sigarette spente in una pozza.

Fra lame d'acqua buia
non ha echi
il tuo ridere rosso:
apre misteri
di primitiva umanità.

Fra poco
urlerà la sirena della fabbrica:
curvi profili in corsa
schiuderanno
laceri varchi nella nebbia.

Oscure
masse di travi: e il peso
del silenzio tra case non finite
grava con noi
sulla fanghiglia,
ai piedi
dell'ultimo fanale.

19 gennaio 1936

Outskirts

Embers flash in the darkness:
　　two cigarettes
　　　　　　hiss
　　in a puddle.

Between blades
　　of black water
　　　　　　echoless
　　　　your red laugh: opens
　　　　　　mysteries
　　　of primitive
　　humanity.

Soon
　　the factory siren
　　will howl:
hustling bent profiles
　　　will open
　　　　　　ragged holes
　　　in the fog.

Dark masses,
　　　　beams:
　　　the burden
　　of silence
amidst unfinished houses
　　　　weighs
　　　　　with us
　　　in the mud,
　　　at the foot
of the last
lamp post.

Maggio desiderio di morte

Sul monte
un convento di foglie
salva il riso d'azzurri fiori.
E tu férmati pallido sole,
questa tempia
che affonda nel muschio
configgi alla terra,
da' al peso
eternità primaverile.

maggio 1936

May death wish

Mountain
cloister
     of leaves
      redeems
the laughter
of blue flowers.
Stop, pale
        sun
    nail
to the ground
this temple
        downed
    in moss
translate the weight
to eternal
      vernal.

Verginità

Vele solari
col tuo piede scarno
tentavi dal pontile,
raccoglievi
chiare sillabe d'acqua
nella scia delle barche.

Poi un profilo d'alte pietre
franava in lago:

ridendo
offrivi alghe al mio nudo
corpo serale.

26 settembre 1936

Virginity

Solar sails
with your slender
                foot
     you tried
from the quay,
      you gathered
clear syllables
          of water
in the wake of the boats.

Then an elevation
     of tall stones
         collapsed
  in the lake:

laughing
you offered
      seaweed
  to my naked
       dusky
  body.

Sete

Or vuoi ch'io ti racconti
una storia di pesci
mentre il lago s'annebbia?
Ma non vedi
come batte la sete nella gola
delle lucertole sul fogliame trito?
A terra
i ricci morti d'autunno
hanno trafitto le pervinche.
E mordi
gli steli arsi: ti sanguina
già lievemente l'angolo del labbro.
Ed or vuoi
ch'io ti racconti una storia d'uccelli?
Ma all'afa
del mezzogiorno il cuculo feroce
svolazza solo.
Ed ancora
urla tra i rovi il cucciolo perduto:
forse il baio in corsa
con lo zoccolo nero lo colpì
sul muso.

28 aprile 1937

Thirst

Want me to tell you
                a fish story
      as the lake sinks
          in fog?
Don't you see
        how thirst throbs
     in the throats of lizards
         on nibbled leaf?
On the ground
      the rich
    autumnal dead transfix
the periwinkles.
You bite
     burnt stems:
    blood trickles
from the corner of your lip.
Want me to tell you
           a bird story?
     In noon heat the fierce cuckoo
       flits solo.
The lost puppy
      still howls
    in the brambles:
maybe the black-hoofed bay
     broke into a run
   & kicked him
       in the face.

Amor fati

Quando dal mio buio traboccherai
di schianto
in una cascata
di sangue—
navigherò con una rossa vela
per orridi silenzi
ai cratèri
della luce promessa.

13 maggio 1937

Amor fati

When suddenly
           you spill
     out of my dark
       cascade
       of blood—
            red sail
         I cut
      through horrid
   silences
to the crater
of light
      betrothed.

Sera a settembre

Aria di neve ai monti
ora colmi il villaggio di campani,
porte spalanchi al magro
ultimo fieno:

quando ai carri s'aggrappano bambini
e affioran rade, calde per la valle
trasparenze di case illuminate.

Dall'ombra—allora—a me salgono nenie
di zingari accampati sulle strade . . .

Pasturo, 13 settembre 1937

September evening

Snow   mountain   air

       fill the village
               with bells
       fling open doors
          to the gaunt
         late
         hay:

when children
         hang
     on carts
& transparencies
          of lighted
       houses
     flicker on
     scattered,
         warm
through the valley.

Then the winge
         reaches me
     from the shadow
         gypsies
camped by the roads.

Morte di una stagione

Piovve tutta la notte
sulle memorie dell'estate.

A buio uscimmo
entro un tuonare lugubre di pietre,
fermi sull'argine reggemmo lanterne
a esplorare il pericolo dei ponti.

All'alba pallidi vedemmo le rondini
sui fili fradice immote
spiare cenni arcani di partenza—

e le specchiavano sulla terra
le fontane dai volti disfatti.

Pasturo, 20 settembre 1937

Death of a season

It rained all night
        on summer's
memories.

In the dark we left
        inside
a mournful
           thundering
of stones, standing
on the bank we lifted
      torches
        to explore
bridges,
          their danger.

Pale at dawn
        we saw
    swallows
on the lines
        soaked,
            still
spying secret
          farewell
    nods—

& ground-level
      mirrored
   in streams
         their faces
      ravaged.

Nebbia

Se c'incontrassimo questa sera
pel viale oppresso di nebbia
si asciugherebbero le pozzanghere
intorno al nostro scoglio caldo di terra:
e la mia guancia sopra le tue vesti
sarebbe dolce salvezza della vita.
Ma fronti lisce di fanciulle
a me rimproverano gli anni: un albero
solo ho compagno nella tenebra piovosa
e lumi lenti di carri mi fanno temere,
temere e chiamare la morte.

27 novembre 1937

Fog

Suppose we met tonight
on a path
      sunk
    in fog
puddles would dry
   round our warm patch
of earth:
     my cheek
against your clothes
     sweet
deliverance
from life.
     But the girls—
their smooth brows chide
my age: a tree
       my sole mate
in the rainy darkness
  slow lights
     wagons
      make me
   scared,
   scared
& summon
     death.

Capodanno

Se le parole sapessero di neve
stasera, che canti—
e le stelle
che non potrò mai dire . . .

Volti immoti s'intrecciano fra i rami
nel mio turchino nero:
osano ancora,
morti ai lumi di case lontane,
l'indistrutto sorriso dei miei anni.

Madonna di Campiglio,
31 dicembre 1937–1 gennaio 1938

New year

If words might
                know
                snow
        tonight,
what songs —
                & stars
I couldn't ever
        utter . . .

Motionless
        faces mesh
    amongst the branches
in my blue black:
                dead
in the lights of distant houses
    they still dare
                the undying
                smile
    of my years.

Certezza

Tu sei l'erba e la terra, il senso
quando uno cammina a piedi scalzi
per un campo arato.
Per te annodavo il mio grembiule rosso
e ora piego a questa fontana
muta immersa in un grembo di monti:
so che a un tratto
—il mezzogiorno sciamerà coi gridi
dei suoi fringuelli—
sgorgherà il tuo volto
nello specchio sereno, accanto al mio.

9 gennaio 1938

Certainty

You are
        grass and earth,
   the feeling
of a barefoot walk
through a turned-up field—
        for you
I knotted my red
                apron
& now bend over
   this stream
        mute, immersed
        in a womb
of mountains:
knowing that
suddenly—noon
                will swarm
        with cries
        finches—
   your face
        will well up
in the calm mirror,
        next to mine.

Luci libere

È un sole bianco che intenerisce
sui monumenti le donne di bronzo.

Vorresti sparire alle case, destarti
ove trascinano lenti carri
sbarre di ferro verso la campagna—

ché là pei fossi infuriano bambini
nell'acqua, all'aurora
e vi crollano immagini di pioppi.

Noi, per seguir la danza
di un vecchio organo
correremmo nel vento gli stradali . . .

A cuore scalzo
e con laceri pesi
di gioia.

27 gennaio 1938

In broad daylight

A white sun
            softens
      bronze
            women
on the monuments.

You'd like to vanish
            indoors
      wake up
where slow wagons
            drag iron bars
      to the country—

because there in the ditches
            babies
                  rage
      in the water
      at dawn
                  & images
      of poplars
                  collapse.

Keeping up
            with the dance
      of an old organ
                  we'd dash
down windy roads . . .

Barefoot
            heart
      & tattered
      loads
of joy.

Pan

Mi danzava una macchia di sole
tepida sulla fronte,
c'era ancora un frusciare di vento
tra foglie lontanissime.

Poi venne
solo: la schiuma di queste onde di sangue
e un martellio di campane nel buio,
giù nel buio per vortici intensi,
per rossi colpi di silenzio—allo schianto.

Dopo
riallacciavano le formiche
nere fila di vita tra l'erba
vicino ai capelli
e sul mio—sul tuo volto sudato
una farfalla batteva le ali.

27 febbraio 1938

Pan

A patch of sun
        danced with me
              tepid
   on the brow,
wind still rustling
the farthest leaves.

He came later
   alone: the foam
of these waves
          blood
& a hammering of bells in the dark
        deep in the dark
through violent whirlpools
through red rams
           of silence—
     at the ripping.

Afterwards
ants stitched
        a living
   black thread
in the grass near our hair
& on my—
       on your
   dewy face
a butterfly
parted
its wings.

Via dei Cinquecento

Pesano fra noi due
troppe parole non dette

e la fame non appagata,
gli urli dei bimbi non placati,
il petto delle mamme tisiche
e l'odore—
odor di cenci, d'escrementi, di morti—
serpeggiante per tetri corridoi

sono una siepe che geme nel vento
fra me e te.

Ma fuori,
due grandi lumi fermi sotto stelle nebbiose
dicono larghi sbocchi
ed acqua
che va alla campagna;

e ogni lama di luce, ogni chiesa
nera sul cielo, ogni passo
di povere scarpe sfasciate

porta per strade d'aria
religiosamente
me a te.

27 febbraio 1938

Via dei Cinquecento

Too much
      unsaid
   lies
   heavy
 between us two

hunger unfed
howling babies unsoothed
the consumptive mother's breast
& the stench—
stench of rags, excrement, corpses
snaking through dark corridors—

a hedge
      groaning
  in the wind
between me and you.

But outdoors
two huge lamps
         steadfast
  beneath misty stars
betoken open floodgates
     water
for the countryside;

& every blade
      of light
every church
black against the sky,
every step
in sorry-worn-out shoes

bears me
    to you
  religiously
  through streets
       of air.

Mattino

In riva al lago azzurro della vita
son corpi le nuvole bianche
dei figli carnosi del sole:

già l'ombra è alle spalle, catena
di monti sommersi.

E a noi petali freschi di rosa
infioran la mensa e son boschi
interi e verdi di castani smossi
nel vento delle chiome:

odi giunger gli uccelli?

Essi non hanno paura
dei nostri volti e delle nostre vesti
perché come polpa di frutto
siamo nati dall'umida terra.

Pasturo, 10 luglio 1938

Morning

On the shore of the blue lake
             of living
                      white clouds
          are bodies
the sun's
fleshy sons:

already a shadow has lain
             right over
             your shoulder
                      a chain
of submersed mountains.

Chez nous
fresh rose petals
          deck the table
the woods are intact
                      & green
     with chestnut trees
     their leaves
stirred in the wind:

d'you hear the birds arrive?

They're not afraid
          of our faces
          our clothes
     like pulpy fruit
we're birthed
from moist earth.

Letters

Antonia Pozzi, 1929

To Antonio Maria Cervi

Milan, 11 January 1930

Piccolo mio, my little one,
  I would have written to you at once, yesterday; but I wasn't
capable of it. The pure and most sweet reality you've offered to
my love-thirsty youth swathes and disperses my tormented rever-
ies; your beloved voice pours silence over my broken words.
  You are truly the angel of my life.
  Little one, I never kissed a man before you. For three years
during my adolescence, I was desperately in love with an opera
singer. We would arrange to meet in the Galleria or in Piazza
della Scala; we strolled back and forth; I a thin, gangly young
girl, he a prosperous gentleman, hair dyed blonde, fingers full
of rings. Every day, perhaps as a joke, he propositioned me in the
most dodgy ways: I didn't understand then, but I guessed, and
fled, after those meetings, with an indescribable feeling of bitter-
ness and disgust.
  And yet I didn't leave off: I needed only to see him on the
stage, once, and the castle of my vexed daydreams loomed up
again, gigantic, like a nightmare.
  In October of 1927, I knew he wasn't going to sing at La Scala
that year, but he would appear at the Opera in Rome. (I must be
fated to take trips to the capital.)
  And then . . . then I had the most unpleasant encounter of my
life.
  And what did you do, you brute, to my poor *animula,* my
little soul, crumpled and wrinkled like a withered leaf? You gen-
tly opened my animula, with your holy hands; you stroked it,
widened it to encompass the most immense things, stretched it
out beneath the sun, so that the sun might warm it and distill
its fragrances. And I, I who had begun to look at you simply as a
whim, perhaps only to forget about *the other guy* . . . oh, piccolo:
it was life, you know, *la vita nuova,* the new, true life, the un-
known light so often invoked, descending upon me, from you,
in broad waves. . . .
  Love, my love, I used to dream repeatedly of giving and re-
ceiving so many kisses, in my adolescence, when I was alone and
naughty: but these dreams were turbid, like a delirium.
  The other day, while I was kissing you, my soul was limpid,
like a cup of water.

So pure were my lips that I didn't even feel them blanch. I felt so safe, so calm: like a mamma kissing her sick baby.

Piccolo, yesterday when you left me, you said: "If you change, I would suffer in silence." Don't say that again to me: that sentence hurts me so badly. I'm all yours, forever. I'm likely to die before I forget you. I feel so strong, now, against everything: nothing, nothing can ever separate us.

No one, I think, not even my father and mother have the right to cut off the paths of two souls: and if these two paths join, if these two are but one life, no one has the right, no one should have the power to divide them.

If you summon me, before too many years pass, I shall free myself from all the hands that want to hold me back, and put my life in yours alone. And if you would rather not have me with you, if you would like our love to remain the flicker of two flames, at a distance, I shall tend my lamp till the moment I doze off forever. I too, as you told me, want only what you want.

Piccolo, the scent of your hair lingered on the armchair where you sat: last night I was nosing around for it. It remained on my hands too, although now gone, and will soon vanish from my clothes. But from my soul the scent of you can't fade away.

I have been wanting to ask you something: what should I call you? Should I too call you Antonello? Tell me when you write. Write me a long letter, please: tell me anything at all about yourself, about your life, even if it seems banal to you. I read all your words with the same excitement.

Within 7 or 8 days you shall be able to send me the famous book—without risking any trouble; and I shall play that children's game: "water, water—fire, fire." . . . Joy, my joy, I have never been so happy for so long!

I am strong; I am well; I feel like studying.

And now, down on the street, a barrel organ grinds out its cloying grace notes, now . . . now I can't tell whether I feel like laughing or crying.

Poppet, sheer dear: my gentle kiss on your lips, my fondest caress of your hair.

With infinite love

your Antonia

To Tullio Gadenz

Milan, 29 January 1933

Dear Tullio,

So, you have been on high. On your superhuman mountains. And you have seen the stars bloom from the depths and you have felt immortalized, beyond every earthly, nocturnal shade. Like the kingly boy who climbed "up the steps of the Sass Maor—at the eternal frontiers—of its heavenly blue realms."

Seriously, I was thinking of you, now that so many days have dropped their ashes on my snow-brightened memories, now that nothing, perhaps, of your human appearance is still alive in me, except your eyes (so kind and intent, so soulful). And as I thought of you I imagined your life as that of a little prince in a fairy-tale realm: a realm to which my soul would often migrate from the circumscribed world, although it can't always, it mustn't always; yet a realm whose presence can be perceived, beyond the veil of bitter sorrows, and one feels miraculously restored by it. For not because of some abstract argument, Tullio, but because of an experience that burns through my entire life, because of an innate, irrevocable adherence to the most profound existence, I believe in poetry. And I live on poetry the way veins live on blood. I know what it means to summon up your entire soul in your eyes so as to drink in the soul of things, humble things, tortured in their gigantic silence, feeling them to be mute sisters to our pain. Because for me God is and can be nothing other than an Infinity, which, in order to be perennially alive and there-fore more Infinite, is incessantly materialized in determinate forms which at every turn are shattered by the urgency of the di-vine flow and then are remoulded to express and materialize the Life that, unexpressed, would be annihilated.

Now, you see that such a God cannot be called upon or prayed to or distanced from us to elicit our adoration. He can only be *lived* deeply, whereupon He is the eye that permits us to see, the voice that sings in us, the love as well as the pain that makes us insomniac. And this our irremediable life, our fatal path, in which we constantly realize—create, so to speak—God in our hearts is nothing other than the wait for the momentous day when the shell shatters and the divine spark leaps out anew in the bosom of the great Flame. Where can we have a more immediate sense of this God who doesn't allow himself to be cut off from life than in those moments when the struggle grows keen between the spirit and the forms that shackle the flow? Is not poetry one of those moments? Do not the need and the labor required to hurl the dream into words perhaps pay for the ecstatic joy of the dream? And might not a spark of the divine absolute gleam in the labor of that act? I believe that our task, while we await God's return, is precisely this: discovering as much God as we can in this life, creating Him, making Him leap out like a spark from the collision between our souls and things (poetry and pain) and from our mutual contact (charity, fraternity). This is why poetry is sacred to me, Tullio; this is why the sacrifices that have stolen so much of my youth are sacred to me; this is why the souls that I feel, beyond any earthly garment, in communion with my soul are sacred to me.

I have suffered so much, Tullio; and if I don't suffer today as I once did, it is perhaps because—as I have already told you—my soul blanches and thinks that late twilight has fallen. Within me is a garden of dead flowers, killed trees: and the dead flowers keep vigil with me, sad as an old mamma near the grave of her only child.

And yet, believe me, if a ray of sunlight can still clear a path in the fog, it shines only where I feel that my heart has touched another heart, where I feel that I have lightened the heavy hour with another life. It also shines, as I said, wherever my intent eyes manage to evoke the soul of things—and compel them to pour out their suffering over my own sorrow.

In a word, I see no other salvation, for the continuation of my life, but to extend my hands and summon things and souls as sisters, who issue from shadow, who huddle around what little fire remains and warms, waiting for nightfall, while outside is icy winter.

Tullio, I have written about so much to you! And how grey, basically, how heavy, how different it is from the sky-blue bliss that you bring back, at night, when you descend from the peaks!

But you must forgive me; because all these things, finally, have one meaning: that I am so happy, Tullio, to have your friendship. I would like you to feel how much frankness, how much spiritual purity lies in my closeness to you. I would like you to think of me truly as a sister, who is here, heart open, arms outstretched, to delight in your joys and to suffer your pains.

Dear Tullio, don't think that a pitiful solitude gathers around your song. Do you know how many creatures emerge from the depths, as it grows dark, and listen ecstatic to the birds' secret melodies?

In fact, continuing the image, I like to picture myself as a timid deer that traces tiny footprints in the snow, at the base of a huge fir tree, from whose branches a tiny songbird's notes rise towards the stars.

And now I must leave you, Tullio. Because I know that this conversation, woven slowly on the woof of a silvery-grey day (rain and snow together—it's Sunday—intense silence), risks annoying you.

Send me another gift soon, one that is reminiscent of sky-blue, like your last letter, and don't forget your new little sister.

With affection,

Antonia Pozzi

P.S. Let me know if you're still planning to come to Milan. In any case, before leaving San Martino, send me your address in Rome too. Don't let me lose track of you! Thanks.

To Elvira Gandini

Pasturo, 8 August 1933

My dear dear Elvira,

Please forgive my silence all these days. I was waiting to receive copies of my photographs so I could send them to you. They don't amount to much, but they can be useful in filling out memories. How I spent my time till now I couldn't tell you: I know only that the more the days at Breil recede, the more they seem to me — beyond all measure — a blue fissure in a uniform life. I've read and reread Guido Rey's book: the final chapters are marvelous. The precipitous descent from the peak to the shelter, at night, is unforgettable; so is the description of the chasms at Tiefenmatten. A little later, the malady of Cervino seized me, and I peopled the bourgeois somnolence of these mountains with summits, ridges, sheer walls. Saturday night, beneath a moon that flooded the entire valley, I climbed the Grigna, and I was up there before dawn, alone on the peak, under the icy smile of the last stars. Little by little, as my intent eyes penetrated the mist, I saw *our* Cervino rising from the night, summoning the first rays of sunlight, gilding itself with them. Then I thought: I want to cover a great distance, I want to learn how to avoid tiring myself and train with all my might so that I can at least climb as far as the cabin and see a sunset and a dawn from that height. And while I was there, motionless, on the dew-soaked grass, rosy in the very first glimmer of sunlight, and no sound reached me other than the bells, driven aloft in waves, I thought of our evenings in Breil, of the voice of your harmonica speaking slowly to the shepherds' lamps on the mountain, with the stars rising from the snowcaps and bedding down amidst the rocks.

Thanks again, Elvira, for those evenings. Thanks for all your kindness. I would have liked to send you a few pieces of mine, dedicated to you, yet it's strange: nothing stirs in my soul these days but notes and chords of themes that remain remote, confused. Still nothing from the experiences at Breil. And yet . . . "un jour viendra." Please write to me about yourself: send me that piece of yours I couldn't read on the way back. But don't think anymore about *ending*. For the mountain is the first thing that teaches us to *endure*, notwithstanding the bruises and lacerations. May the new mountain lavish strength and sunlight on you, may all your days be calm.

Antonia

P.S. I'm not going to Portorose. I shall stay here all summer.

To Antonio Maria Cervi

Milan, 11–15 February 1934

Antonello,

I didn't hear your words this morning. I heard only your voice. I didn't understand the nasty things. I understood that you *are,* still, alive, beyond me; that *there is* still something on which I can focus, beyond this ugly, miserable world.

We can choose solitude, the most profound solitude, provided that we carry within ourselves something *other* than ourselves, something to which we can talk and pray, something we can believe in, apart from ourselves.

You are in me, still. The one and only light, steady as an altar, growing brighter in proportion to the dark stains that multiply around it. Don't tell me that I lied to you. If I have given you more sorrow than joy, if I yielded to the sorrow of others and asked you to renounce, not our love, but the realization of our love, if I couldn't fulfill any of your expectations of me—rest assured—I gave you *everything* I *could.*

Don't tell me that I haven't loved you.

I was sixteen when I saw you. Tomorrow I turn twenty-two. From then till now I have lived only for you. You can't deny it. You can't deny an entire life with a single word. Above all, you can't destroy, in me, what was born only in your name, in the light of your soul: my soul as a woman, a mamma. Antonello, let me put it like this: even if our child won't be born, if *no* child will be born to me, *ever,* even if you feel that I alone, deliberately, killed your baby, you don't realize that in every baby's face I see only *that* face and *those* little hands, you don't know what I feel—only a woman could understand—but I swear to you, Antonello, even if I was wrong, if I failed, I don't profane the sacred when I utter to myself, prayer-like, the name that *he* should have.

Only in his name, Antonello, do I *beg you* not to deny my entire life. For our love was truly *all* my life. At the start, I was no more than a naughty girl. Do you remember? I began to *live* with you: you gave me my first good books, made me think about God. Then, day by day, it was as if you gave blood to this creature of yours, my soul. I learned to look at things with your eyes. Then I would always love and endure them by evaluating them with you, the image of you. You don't know, Antonello.

But if you tell me that you never believed me, if you say that my entire life has been false, I feel like someone who, after bringing flowers to a grave for many years, believing it to be his mother's, is suddenly told that his mother isn't there, she's buried elsewhere, far away.

So, be careful: it isn't simply a question of getting something wrong. On that something a whole life is woven, a whole world. If it collapses, darkness falls, and you can't tell what will happen.

You see, Antonello: first I *knew* that so much evil exists in the world, but "a priori": I had never touched it with my hands, had never *seen* it in the eyes of those I took for brothers. Now, I have *seen* it. And I am entirely on my own, cut off from everyone, trying to save myself and others.

I have so much compassion for everyone.

But you know, the more I saw evil hatching, the more I thought: "There is *one man* in the world who *is not* like this. And I am *his*. No one in the world is more *pure* than he. And God has given him *to me*. So, *what* can an entire life of emptiness matter, if I enjoy the grace of your face, even for a short while? Does not a single moment of your purity stretch out like an eternal life before us impure wretches?"

It was as if the whole world had sunk in the sands, but you remained, high above, on an island of lilies, and you lifted me into your light; as in that fresco by Fra Angelico, at San Marco, where the Saints are arrayed below, corporeal, heavy, dark, and the Virgin is kneeling above, almost in fear, swathed in white veils, as the Lord moves to crown her from on high.

Do you remember, Antonello?

When I wanted to kiss you with impure lips, you gently moved me away, and told me: "The kisses will hurt you today, Babydoll."

I *believe*, I *know,* that no man *ever* spoke such holy words to a woman. You alone, Antonello, you alone. For it was God speaking in you, *wanting to save me* through you. You can't destroy yourself in my life, because you were the word of God in me, the promise of my redemption.

It is not true that you don't believe me. There is more of you in me than what I am, and you know all of me: you see through space, through the years, past this face, which people think they know, past my many false self-images, which wander down streets and enter men's houses to laugh and tell lies: you are in the depths of me, in conversation with my one and only true self, the self that has been yours. You believe me when I tell you that, for me, everything is just as before, more so than it was before; I have not been and shall never be any other man's but yours. Moreover:

my soul, not only my heart, my mind, my way of thinking and living, my human dignity, will always be what you have seen and wished them to be.

You believe me because you were with me, last year, in the garden at Caserta, gathering cyclamen, then glimpsed on the threshold in Santa Maria del Pianto and at Siracusa, along the dark and deep Anapo.

You were with me for days, on the slopes of Monte Grappa, when I saw that huge mountain for the first time: I gazed at it, open beneath the sky like a white altar; I searched for rose bushes and cypresses on the hills. I saw the houses at Crespano, in the distance.

Don't tell me that you don't believe me.

I didn't ask you for anything, Antonello. If for a moment I desired to hear your voice once more, it wasn't to ask you to suffer and to fight for me again. It was to thank you for what you were to me, especially for what you still are, what you *now* are and will always be to me. You were the first person who spoke of light to me: you are the only one in whom I believed, in whom I believe. You are *proof* that good exists, here, beyond the intrigues, the lies, the sin.

I wanted to tell you, Antonello, that if a glimmer of faith survives in me, it is my memory of you, my respect for and veneration of you. I wanted to ask for your forgiveness, with the soul I possess today, because yesterday I didn't love enough the most holy and hidden part of you.

But I didn't suffer enough, then, and I couldn't penetrate your heart entirely.

Now I see more clearly. Now, from a distance, I see so many things I didn't see when I was in your arms. I have only these regrets: that I gave you so little of myself, the most wretched and blind part; and that today I am unable to give you my more capacious soul, a soul that is less unworthy of you. But I know that the more the years pass, the more ruins and sorrows accumulate around us, the brighter your image will shine over my heart, and the louder your name will resound. And perhaps this won't be love any longer: perhaps it will be greater than love—the comprehension of God in this life.

Antonello, if I wanted to hear your voice again, it would be only to ask you to forgive me, once more, for all the pain that befell you because of me. I would also want to tell you that all your tears, all our tears were not in vain: that my soul isn't lost, that you aren't lost in me. You will be my salvation in eternity.

And it is not true that you don't believe me.

Perhaps to *feel* the untruth of this notion that you don't believe me, you need only think of a June morning and a broad sweep of poppies. When I told you that I wanted to bestow all the light in the world upon *him,* with my thoughts, before he was born, they *were not* merely words.

The *weight* of his "invisible coffin" *is not,* now, merely a word.

It *is not* merely a word if I tell you that the good and the bad, the meaning of my entire life resides forever in that *weight.*

Antonello, forgive all my faults, if you can. I would like you to enjoy all the happiness that I haven't given you. I would like the Lord to bless and protect you always.

I feel as if I can still sign myself, with spiritual purity and confidence,

your *Antonia*

To Vittorio Sereni

Pasturo, 20 June 1935

Vitto dear,

I wanted to write to you as soon as I got back, last Thursday, because I really didn't like that "spectral" look on your face, your restless tension. But then up here, with Paolo Treves and Remo Cantoni, my time just flew. Today, finally, I'm taking advantage of the solitude (Remo went to Milan with his mother to see about her passport; Paolo has been gone a few days now). I would like to write at length to compensate somehow for losing the lovely custom of your daily visits, for which I am so nostalgic. I don't know: I have lived for so many years now and can't make any sense whatsoever of my life. Here I am, in this interval of silence, like a veil of water suspended over a rock in the midst of a cascade, waiting to fall headlong again. It is as if I had cut off all ties with the outside world in favor of a world that has already received a death date, that may not even exist as an independent world, that may be no more than the death throes of a long period in my life. You can't imagine the relentlessness of daily living: being compared day in and day out, measuring one's differences against the ruler of petty material realities, as it minces feelings, as it buries idealized concepts. What an intense trial by fire. It can help, as you know, and it can be a blessing, if it serves to dismantle the idols. But what a collision with the earth.

So many frightening abysses gape between Remo and me. In taste, in sensibility; in morality, above all. And this is especially terrifying: my absolute lack of adaptability to real life. The oneness of my being is utterly shattered whenever I am borne out of the unreal atmosphere in which solitude has reared me. Yet I don't know how right it is for Remo to say that he wants to make a real woman of me: I believe and fear that a real woman I shall never be, that in fact, by trying—unsuccessfully—to be such a woman, I would wind up losing that part of me which is the most true and least banal. Perhaps my destiny is truly to write beautiful books of fairy tales for children I will never have.

More than ever I feel like Tonia Kröger, as poor Gianni Manzi called me and as we felt—in toto—that night at Alberto Mondadori's. Do you remember, Vittorio? That night I resisted only because I had you close by; I shall remember for the rest of my life what you were to me in those hours. But once you told me something that troubles me terribly today: you told me that I am very noble, that I *don't know* what vulgarity is. If only you could see me today, Vittorio, see the tremendous fissure that has opened wide within me, the collapse that has occurred. On one side is the Antonia of the poems and good principles, on the other a being without will, lacking a center, who listens to the most brutal remarks without reacting, and when the eyes that face her turn cynical—no longer fraternal or compassionate—she doesn't stand up, doesn't leave, but remains as if hypnotized, waiting for the caresses that she knows will be given to her—not out of pity —but as a joke, a stupid joke that is utterly worthless, but can cost a life.

Vittorio, you are the only person to whom I dare confide this shame. I don't know what will happen. This letter strikes me as the last will and testament of the Antonia you knew, the scream of the water before it tumbles down the rock face. But then it isn't, certainly not. Because I am too cowardly to go the distance. And the player is, after all, too serious to want the game to be deadly. Still, I am terrified by this utter disintegration of my self, this caving in without any buttresses, and I don't see any salvation. Perhaps if we could be neighbors again, nurturing a common belief in so many precious things, the situation would be different. Did you read Civinini's novel *Bisogno di una sorella* [The need for a sister]? This is what you have been to me: a being of a different sex, yet so close that my blood seemed to flow in his veins, I could look in his eyes without anxiety, he is neither above nor facing me, but at my side, walking with me on the same plain. With you I experienced poor Gianni's death one night; a train journey on a Sunday lulled our melancholies, at once like and unlike. One day we listened to *June in January,* and your poetry made me weep, not perhaps because of what you said, but because of the throbbing world it caused to grow inside me, with the certainty that only your poetry can create this world in me, and this world alone is my true and purest life.

Vitto caro, you're sitting for your examinations now, and I don't dare ask you to reply: my greatest need is for you to talk to me about the outside world, to save me from this insidious, ephemeral world whose violent arms bear me away from myself. Next week I may come to Milan for a day and we can meet. If before then you can write me a line—just a single line—I would be so grateful: I really need your friendship, caro Vittorio. Forgive me if I'm so clingy. Tell me about yourself, about Milan,

Brescia: send me what you have done, even if unfinished. I haven't written anything. I'm just like Tonio Kröger in the storm.

Addio, Vittorio. Give my warm regards to your mamma and don't forget me.

I embrace you with great affection.

Antonia

To Maria Cavagna Sangiuliani

Pasturo, 18 July 1938

My dear dear precious Grandma,
    I am deeply moved, nearly have a lump in my throat. It is
always like this: you are asked for a glass of water and you give,
give like a stream, like an inexhaustible spring. Your childhood
is all here, in my hands, and it speaks to my imagination like an
entire novel already written. If, on the one hand, I regret mak-
ing you toil away like this, on the other I am happy that you have
entrusted your memories to the pen, memories that are so valu-
able and marvelous because of their vividness, the sense of vastness
and calm, and the rich Lombard life that runs through them.
Here is your entire personality, so profoundly realistic, cleaving
to things and feelings, and at the same time filled with poetry.
Many thanks, my great treasure. Now—you see—I am almost
more frightened than before: how shall I render all this without
distorting it too much? What proportions should the book have?
Within what boundaries, with what kinds of foreshortening
should it be constructed? The architecture is such a complicated
thing! Sometimes I imagine it becoming the history of *Three
Houses*: Oscasale, Zelada, Pasturo (I would have you come live here
with us, at the end, understand? With your daughter—a war
widow? I still haven't decided—and your grandson, who will per-
haps be a little like me, but everything is still vague, forming
and fading like clouds before a storm). From here, from the sour
green pastures, a broad tawny river of nostalgia flows down to-
wards the plain and its gathered riches, towards the long songs of
winnowing beneath the sun, towards the other two abandoned
houses. And then everything would be resolved in the encounter
between your grandson and a girl of humble origins, a native
of that very area, of the plain, yet raised by her own efforts: at first,
a rural schoolteacher, then a teacher in the city, perhaps a nurse
as well (he'll meet her in a hospital); a creature who knows the
poor at close hand and feels a silent yet active pity for them, a
woman who carries about herself the fragrant goodness of the
countryside and at the same time an energy in which *he,* your
grandson, believes that he recognizes his beloved grandmother in
her youth. Do you see, dear Grandma, how the imagination gal-
lops apace? And always it leads me towards more democratic con-
structions, towards the simple, elementary sense of the land and
its poor people.

I realize that the life of the city, of luxury, of movement hasn't left any trace on me, holds no importance for me, I could lose it overnight without uttering the faintest ouch! What I cannot lose is this village and this house, the floral cotton costumes that are more beautiful than all the "toilettes." I am already thinking of inspecting Oscasale and Soresina in the fall to experience the landscape in person. Then I shall have to learn about farming: flax, rice, wheat, and corn; when they are sown, what stages of growth they undergo, what colors they turn, when and how they are harvested. I shall also study many newspapers from various periods. And above all I shall come to listen to you chatter away, and we can hatch lovely plots together. Meanwhile, if you have the time and inclination, you and Aunt Luisa (to whom I also send my enthusiastic thanks) should proceed with that chronological table, which is very precious. I would also like some details about life in the school, the sisters, the schedules and routines during the day. And then . . . then, should the mood take you, let your pen flow, since you are undoubtedly more clever and able than I am, and you always select what works so well. Two words about my health: it's good and improves all the time. Tomorrow Papà leaves for Cannes and the French Riviera (about ten days) and on 4 August we shall all be at Mirsurina. Mamma is just fine, and so is Aunt Ida. Did you know that we have another dog? A shepherd puppy two months old: he's a beauty! But now I have run out of space. A big kiss to Aunt Luisa and a hundred to you.

Antonia

A lodge in the Dolomites. Undated.
Photograph by Antonia Pozzi.

Notes

The Italian texts of Antonia Pozzi's poems are reproduced from the definitive collection, *Parole* (Words; Milan: Garzanti, 1998), edited by Alessandra Cenni and Onorina Dino, who worked primarily from the poet's notebooks and the copies in the possession of her friend Lucia Bozzi. The letters are translated from the same editors' collection of Pozzi's correspondence, *L'età delle parole è finita: Lettere, 1927–1938* (The age of words has ended; Milan: Rosellina Archinto, 1989).

Cenni and Dino's edited volumes include a collection of Pozzi's prose, *Diari* (Milan: Scheiwiller, 1988), and a collection of poems and letters by Pozzi and Vittorio Sereni, *La giovinezza che non trova scampo: poesie e lettere degli anni trenta* (The youth that finds no escape; Milan: Scheiwiller, 1995). Pozzi's thesis was published as *Flaubert: La formazione letteraria (1830–1856)* (Milan: Garzanti, 1940).

I have learned much about Pozzi's poetry from Rebecca West's essay in *Italian Women Writers: A Biobibliographical Sourcebook,* edited by Rinaldina Russell (Westport, Conn.: Greenwood, 1994) and from Catherine O'Brien's anthology, *Italian Women Poets of the Twentieth Century* (Dublin: Irish Academic Press, 1996). For bibliographies of critical commentary on Pozzi's work, see Cenni and Dino's edition of the poetry and West's essay.

The information provided in my introduction and in the following notes relies to a large extent on the work of Pozzi's editors. The notes are intended to illuminate the editing of her poetry and to identify people and places that figure in the poems and letters.

Page 3. *Se le mie parole potessero (If my words could be)*
This dedication opens the first notebook of Pozzi's poems.

Page 4. *Giacere (Lying)*
The harbor town of Santa Margherita is a resort on the Ligurian coast, east from Genoa.

Page 6. *Innocenza (Innocence)*
Pozzi's father struck out the version of this poem in her notebooks, although it remains legible. It also exists in two identical manuscript versions on loose sheets.

Page 10. *Copiatura (Copying)*
Dedicated to Antonio Maria Cervi.

Page 16. *Nostalgia (Nostalgia)*
Kingston is a town on the outskirts of London, southwest of the city. This poem was written during the English trip that Pozzi's parents arranged for her in an effort to break off her relationship with Cervi.

Page 18. *Grido (Scream)*
Pozzi enclosed this poem in a letter to Cervi dated 1 March 1932. In that letter she wrote: "On 10 February, at dusk, a few hours after the delirium in which I feared losing you, I wrote this." She then copied out the poem and commented: "My words are verbose, my pain is vacuous aestheticism, I know. But I alone know how my tears burned that day and what terrible void opened inside me at the mere suspicion that you were no longer mine."

Page 22. *Sogno nel bosco (A dream in the forest)*
Pozzi's father included a substantially revised version of this poem in the first selection of her work published in 1939. He changed the abrupt lineation of the second verse paragraph, perhaps expressing his own conservative poetic taste by creating greater continuity:

> A sera—un capriolo
> sbucando dal folto—disegni
> di piccole orme—la neve
> e all'alba gli uccelli—impazziti
> infiorino di canti il vento.

He also deleted the last verse paragraph, where the image of the "Io" ("I") resting "in pace" ("in peace") beneath a tree carries the suggestion of death. And he changed the title to simply "Nel bosco" ("In the forest"), removing any implication that the scene sketched in the poem might somehow be a wishful dream.

Page 26. *Luce bianca (White light)*
A memory of a cemetery that Pozzi visited during her English trip more than a year earlier.

Page 30. *Acqua alpina (Alpine water)*
"Breil" is an older name for the town of Breuil-Cervinia, one of the first Italian ski resorts.

Page 32. *Respiro (Breath)*
Dedicated to Elvira Gandini, whose close friendship with Pozzi began in secondary school. Gandini played the harmonica. During the summer of 1933 they camped together in the mountains, an experience that Pozzi discusses in a letter to Gandini (dated 8 August 1933) included in this volume.

Page 34. *Cervino*
Cervino is the Italian name for the Alpine mountain known as the Matterhorn (4,476 meters above sea level).

Page 42. *La vita sognata (The dreamt life)*
Pozzi's father included a substantially revised version of this poem in the first selection of her work published in 1939. He deleted several lines ("tu cui un'onda bianca / di tristezza cadeva sul volto / se ti chiamavo con labbra impure" and "il ramo morto di tutti i giorni che restano") laden with suggestions of sexuality and death.

Page 44. *La gioia (The joy)*
The Italian word *pupa,* the feminine form rendered in this poem as "babydoll," was Cervi's term of endearment for Pozzi. In a letter to him (dated 11–15 February 1934) included in this volume, she quotes a sentence in which he applies it to her. She herself used the masculine form, *pupo,* in another letter to him included here (dated 11 January 1930). There it has been rendered as "poppet."

Page 64. *Annotta (Darkening)*
The village of San Martino di Castrozzo is a resort in the Dolomites east of Trento.

Page 82. *Don Chisciotte (Don Quixote)*
According to Pozzi's close friend, Lucia Bozzi, this poem was inspired by G. W. Pabst's 1933 film version of Cervantes's novel.

Page 94. *Assenza (Absence)*
The village of Monate, known today as Travedona Monate, is a resort famous for its lake, located near Varese in western Lombardy.

Page 96. *Esclusi (Exclusions)*
Via Caradosso is located in the center of Milan just off Corso

Magenta, where Pozzi's teacher Antonio Banfi lived. Pozzi frequently visited Banfi at his home to discuss her thesis on Flaubert, which she submitted in November 1935.

Page 122. *Sul ciglio (On the edge)*
The Grigna, a mountain west of Pasturo (2,409 meters), recurs in Pozzi's poems and letters.

Page 134. *Commiato (Envoi)*
The village of Misurina is a resort on a lake in the eastern Dolomites (in the region of Alto Adige).

Page 136. *Salita (Ascent)*
The mountains near Misurina include Sorapis (3,205 meters) and Cristallo (3,221 meters), a name that literally means "crystal."

Page 158. *Capodanno (New year)*
The mountain village of Madonna di Campiglio is a resort northwest of Trento.

Page 166. *Via dei Cinquecento*
The street named in the title is located in a working-class quarter on the outskirts of Milan. During 1938, when Pozzi performed social work on a volunteer basis, she visited tenements here where people who had been evicted from their homes took up residence.

Page 173. *To Antonio Maria Cervi* (11 January 1930)
The Galleria, a huge cruciform arcade lined with shops and cafés, and the Piazza della Scalla, the site of the renowned opera house, are located in the center of Milan. Neither the opera singer nor the "famous book" mentioned by Pozzi has been identified. Pozzi and Cervi were in the habit of exchanging books, even after their relationship met with her parents' disapproval. In the summer of 1931, when Pozzi's parents arranged for her to travel to England, she sent Cervi a copy of Shakespeare's *Romeo and Juliet* with the dedication: "To my beloved Antonello, this tale that bears some resemblance to the tale of our love."

Page 175. *To Tullio Gadenz*
Tullio Gadenz, a poet from Trento, published several collections of poems, including *Viandanti* (Wayfarers, 1934) and *Melodie della sera* (Evening melodies, 1939). His work shares certain formal and

thematic features with Pozzi's, notably free verse, striking imagery, and a Romantic interest in the mountains. Yet in terms of Italian poetic trends, Gadenz's poetry is crepuscular, not hermetic: his lacks the modernist form of Pozzi's, its rapid discontinuity, as well as the personal drama that evoked through elliptical references. Here is a typical poem by Gadenz entitled "Settembre" ("September"), along with a close English version:

Come la fronte di un astro	Like the brow of a star
rosa sopra la valle	pink over the valley
splendon le dolomiti;	the Dolomites shine;
ma ai calici	but the autumn's invisible fairies
con funeree	approach the calyxes
labbra s'accostan	with funereal
le fate invisibili dell'autunno	lips
e più forte	and the iron clock
dall'alto della torre batte	strikes more loudly
l'orologio di ferro . . .	from the top of the tower . . .

The word *calici* in the fourth line is a pun, meaning both "calyxes" and "goblets" or "chalices."

Pozzi met Gadenz at San Martino in the winter of 1933, and over the next year she wrote him a number of letters in which she articulated her views about poetry.

Page 178. *To Elvira Gandini*
Guido Rey was a celebrated mountain guide in Valle d'Aosta who wrote several works about climbing. His book, *Il tempo che torna* (Time restored), was published in 1929. A few days after Pozzi wrote this letter, her camping experiences with Gandini inspired several poems, including "Acqua alpina" ("Alpine water"), "Respiro" ("Breath"), and "Cervino." The French expression *un jour viendra* means "a day will come." Portorose, known today as Portoroz, is a resort on the Adriatic coast of Slovenia.

Page 179. *To Antonia Maria Cervi*
This letter is filled with references to moments, places, and issues in Pozzi's relationship with Cervi. The fresco she describes by the fifteenth-century painter Fra Angelico is the *Coronation of the Virgin,* located in a dormitory at the Cloister of San Antonio in the Piazza San Marco in Florence. In April 1933 she traveled to southern Italy, stopping at towns in Campania and Sicily, where such sites as the River Anapo inspired poems. Santa Maria del

Pianto is a church in Naples. Monte Grappa (1,775 meters) in the Veneto was the place where Cervi's brother, the poet Annunzio Cervi, died in battle in 1918. Not only did Pozzi and Cervi often discuss their wish to have a son, but they decided to name him after Cervi's brother. The desire to bear Cervi's child is a recurrent motif in Pozzi's poems as well: see, for instance, "Scena unica" ("One act"), included in this volume.

Page 183. *To Vittorio Sereni*
The Treves brothers, Paolo and Piero, were close friends of Pozzi's to whom she showed her poems. Remo Cantoni, Gianni Manzi, and Alberto Mondadori were fellow students at the University of Milan. For a brief time, Pozzi was romantically involved with Cantoni. Manzi committed suicide in 1935. During that year, the poet Vittorio Sereni became Pozzi's confidant. Sereni published his first collection, *Frontiera,* in 1943. Guelfo Civinini was a fiction writer who collaborated on the libretto for Giacomo Puccini's 1910 opera, *La fanciulla del West (The Girl of the Golden West).*

Page 186. *To Maria Cavagna Sangiuliani*
During June 1938, after undergoing surgery for appendicitis at a Milanese clinic, Pozzi spent a period of convalescence at Pasturo. On 2 July 1938 she wrote to Maria Cavagna Sangiuliani, her maternal grandmother, to request information about the Lombard countryside and to announce her intention to base a historical novel on her grandmother's life. Pozzi described Cavagna as "the Lombard woman par excellence." By 18 July her grandmother had sent her a set of notes. The names *Oscasale* and *Zelada* refer to villas owned by Cavagna's family and located near villages on the River Ticino. Soresina is a town southeast of Milan on the Po plain.

Acknowledgments

My work received help and encouragement from a number of friends and colleagues, especially at a very early stage—when it was most needed. Some read and commented on the selection of Italian texts and on the English versions, spotted weaknesses, and suggested new directions. These readers were Rachel Blau DuPlessis, Susan Howe, Lucia Re, Susan Stewart, and Rebecca West. Richard Howard's appreciation of the translations was gratifying, but his criticisms of Pozzi's poetry I have been pleased to write against, implicitly, both in the translations and in the introduction. Alfredo de Palchi enthusiastically published some of the translations in *Chelsea*. As director of the Sonia Raiziss Giop Foundation, he welcomed an application for a publishing subvention that aided the production of this book. Bradford Morrow created a showcase for Pozzi in *Conjunctions,* editing the translations in the most sensitive and revealing ways.

Grateful acknowledgment is made to the National Endowment for the Arts, which supported my work on the project with a translator's fellowship. The award made me realize, quite unexpectedly, that the translations might appeal to a diverse range of poetic tastes, crossing the boundaries between American poetry readerships. The panel of judges included such poets as Albert Goldbarth, Rachel Hadas, Heather McHugh, and James Tate.

I wish to express my gratitude to the two anonymous readers for Wesleyan University Press who recognized the importance of having Pozzi's poetry in English, who encouraged my experimental translations, and who helpfully commented on the manuscript.

I have also been inspired by the appreciative responses of Barbara Cole, Luigi Fontanella, Jonathan Galassi, Toby Olson, Beth Scroggin, Kevin Varrone and Patricia McCarthy, Rosanna Warren, and the students in my literary translation course at the Universitat de Vic, in Catalunya, where I taught as a Fulbright lecturer in the spring of 1999 and submitted some translations for class discussion.

Marina Guglielmi of the University of Cagliari carefully examined the English versions against her incisive readings of the Italian texts, leading me to rethink lexical and syntactical choices and to make many serendipitous discoveries and improvements.

Onorina Dino, one of Pozzi's editors, patiently answered my queries concerning archival materials and biographical details and enabled me not only to examine the poet's photographs, but to select several for reproduction here. Giuseppe Strazzeri of Arnoldo Mondadori Editore generously shared with me his deep knowledge of twentieth-century Italian poetry, especially Pozzi's milieu and her friendship with Vittorio Sereni. Marie Louise Zarmanian of Garzanti Editore sent me a copy of the second edition of Pozzi's poems. Mary Wardle of the University of Rome La Sapienza directed me to useful information concerning the Italian locations in the texts.

The research for this project was carried out at Bobst Library of New York University, Regenstein Library at the University of Chicago, the Biblioteca Nazionale in Florence, the Biblioteca Nazionale Braidense and the Biblioteca Nazionale degli Studi Manzoniani, both in Milan. The librarians at these sites graciously facilitated my work. I was also aided by the diligent efforts of the Inter-Library Loan Department of Paley Library at Temple University.

I remain indebted to my children, Gemma Leigh and Julius David, as always, for their forbearance and their inspiration.

The dedication reprints the poem "Sala d'espera" by the Catalan writer Francesc Parcerisas, who kindly permitted me to use it. The poem is included in his collection *Natura morta amb nens* (Barcelona: Quaderns Crema, 2000). Martha Tennent Hamilton, who brought the poem to my attention, responded to this project in a special way.

L.V.
Rome–New York City
May 2001

A lodge on Cervino, January 1935. Photograph by Antonia Pozzi.

Library of Congress Cataloging-in-Publication Data
Pozzi, Antonia, 1912–1938.

   Breath : poems and letters / Antonia Pozzi ;
  edited and translated by Lawrence Venuti.

      p. cm. — (Wesleyan poetry)
  Poems in Italian original with English translation.
  ISBN 0-8195-6543-1 (cloth : alk. paper) —
  ISBN 0-8195-6544-X (pbk. : alk. paper)
   1. Pozzi, Antonia, 1912–1938—Translations into English.
  I. Venuti, Lawrence. II. Title. III. Series.

  PQ4835.O78 B74 2002

  851′.912—dc21   2002069176